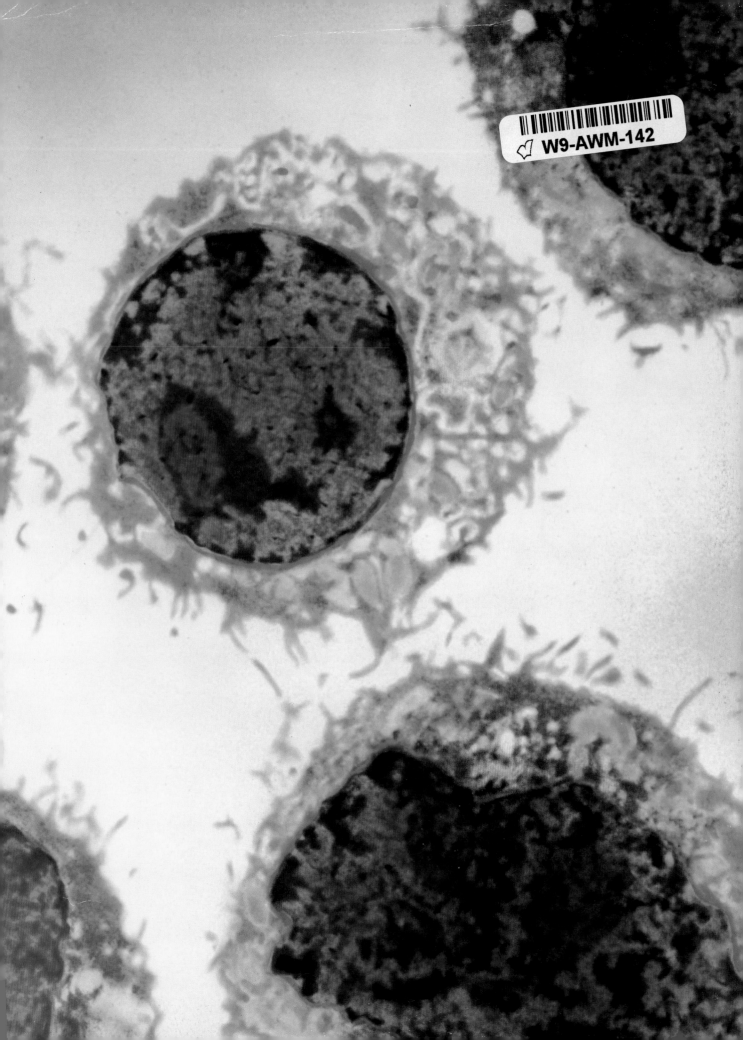

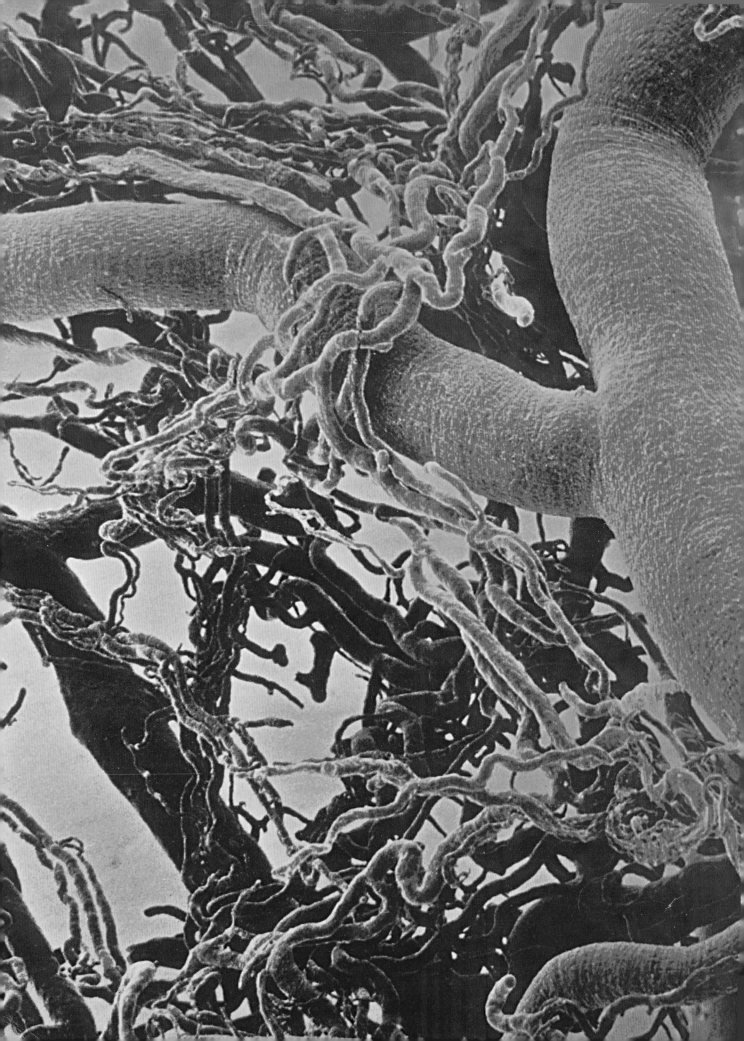

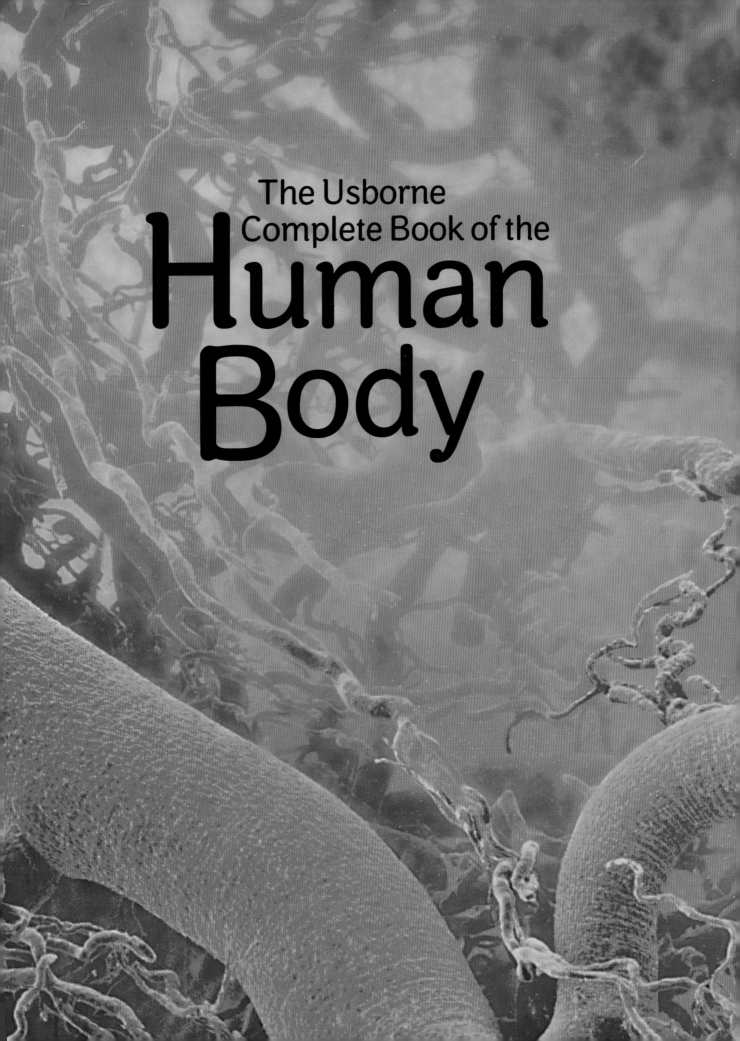

The Usborne
Complete Book of the
Human
Body

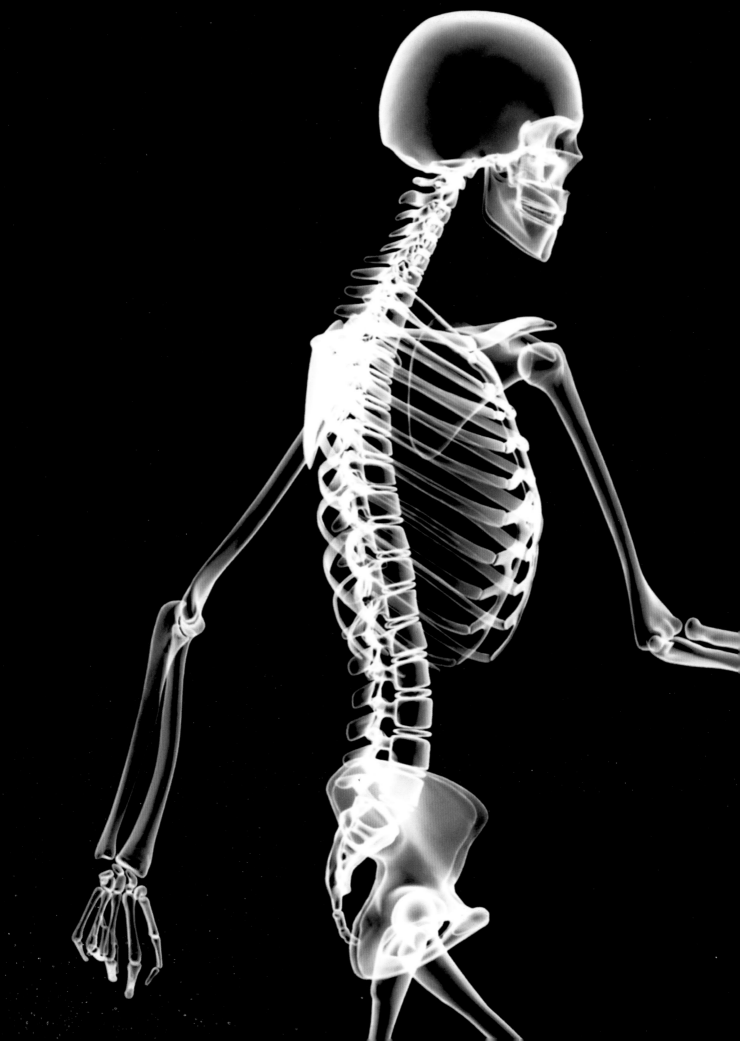

The Usborne
Complete Book of the
Human
Body

Anna Claybourne

Designed by
Stephanie Jones and Stephen Moncrieff

Illustrated by Stephen Moncrieff and Juliet Percival

Scientific consultant: Dr. Visvan Navaratnam,
Department of Anatomy, University of Cambridge, UK
Additional consultants: Dr. Brian Pentland and Dr. Kristina Routh
Edited by Felicity Brooks
American editor: Carrie Armstrong
Art director: Mary Cartwright

Internet links

This book contains descriptions of websites where you can find out more about the human body. To visit the recommended sites, go to the Usborne Quicklinks website at **www.usborne.com/quicklinks** and type the keywords "complete body."

What you can do

Here are some of the things you can do on the websites we recommend:

- View amazing scans of the inside of the human body

- See inside cells and view animations of how they work

- Watch animated movies about the skeleton, blood, digestion, and other body systems

- Try games, puzzles, and quizzes to test your knowledge

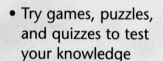

This microscope picture shows a tiny embryo made up of just a few cells on the point of a needle. Over nine months, it will grow into a fully formed human being.

Site availability

The recommended websites are regularly checked and reviewed by Usborne editors and the links at Usborne Quicklinks are updated. If a website closes down, we will replace it with a suitable alternative so you will always find an up-do-date list of sites at Usborne Quicklinks.

Downloadable pictures

Some of the pictures in this book can be downloaded from the Usborne Quicklinks website and printed out for your own personal use. All pictures marked with a ★ are available. They must not be copied or distributed for any commercial purpose.

Internet safety

When using the internet, please follow the internet safety guidelines displayed at the Usborne Quicklinks website at **www.usborne.com/quicklinks**. We recommend that children are supervised while using the internet.

Please note, the content of a website may change at any time and Usborne Publishing is not responsible for the content or availability of any website other than its own.

Microscope and X-ray pictures

Many of the microscope and X-ray images in this book, such as the one on the left, have had extra color added to them to make them clearer. They do not always show the real colors of the human body.

Contents

The X-ray on this page shows the ribs, backbone and collarbone inside a human torso.

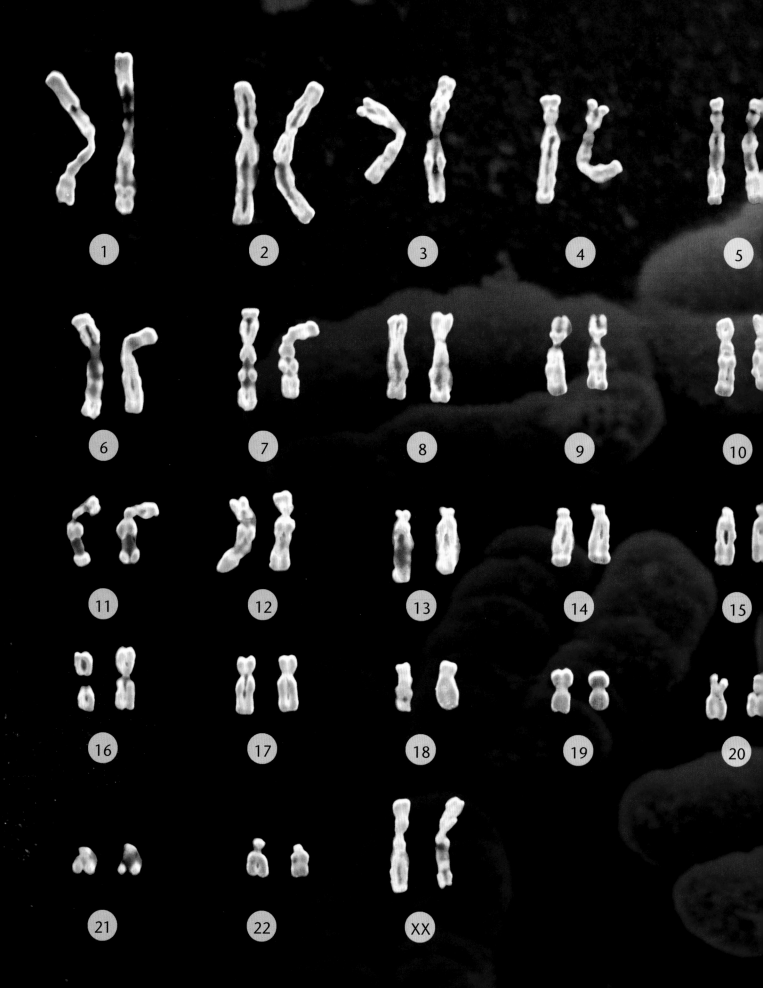

Body Building Blocks

The human body is amazingly complicated. It's made up of hundreds of different organs, tubes, tendons, tissues and other body parts, each with its own job to do. In turn, these parts are made up of millions of microscopic units called cells. Inside cells are the smallest body parts of all – the genes that make us human. They tell cells how to do all the things they need to do to make our bodies work and keep us alive.

Almost every cell in your body contains a set of chromosomes, where your genes are stored. In the set shown on the opposite page, the last pair of chromosomes match, showing that they came from a female. In a male, the last pair of chromosomes do not match, and the pair is called XY instead of XX.

Your amazing body

The human body is an amazing machine. Even though you rarely think about it, your body is always busy. You have dozens of different organs, masses of muscles and bones, miles of blood vessels, millions of cells, and a brain more powerful than any computer, all working together to keep you alive.

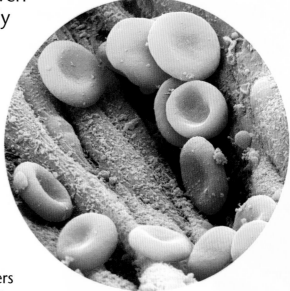

Body parts

Your body is made up of many different parts and substances. Here are the main ones:

• **Organs** are body parts that do a particular job for the rest of your body. For example, your brain controls your body, and your lungs collect the oxygen your body needs.

• **Body tissues** include fat, bone and muscle.

• **Body fluids.** Your body contains many different fluids (liquids). Blood is the most important one. The others include tears, sweat, and stomach juices.

• **Water** makes up 70% of your body. It's found in your blood, and in and around the cells that make up your body.

Red blood cells, an important part of blood, shown at about 3,000 times life-size.

Your brain, eyes and skin are all examples of organs. Skin is the biggest organ of all. It covers and protects your whole body.

BODY SCIENCE:
Fascinating facts

Wherever you see a Body Science box like this, you'll find extra facts such as what archaeologists can tell from old bones, how germs travel and what a phantom limb is.

GOING WRONG:
Body breakdowns

Although your body is amazing, it can go wrong. Look out for these Going Wrong boxes throughout the book. They explain all kinds of body breakdowns and problems, like what causes a heart attack, why teenagers get zits, and what makes you vomit.

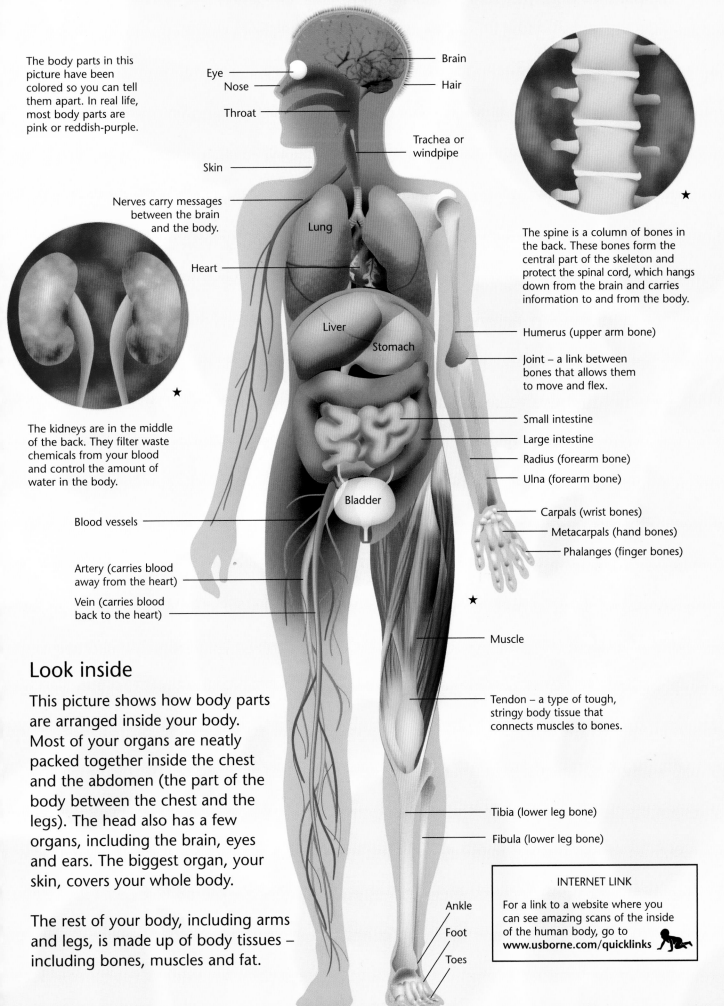

The body parts in this picture have been colored so you can tell them apart. In real life, most body parts are pink or reddish-purple.

Eye
Nose
Throat
Skin
Nerves carry messages between the brain and the body.
Heart
Lung

Brain
Hair
Trachea or windpipe

★

The spine is a column of bones in the back. These bones form the central part of the skeleton and protect the spinal cord, which hangs down from the brain and carries information to and from the body.

Humerus (upper arm bone)

Joint – a link between bones that allows them to move and flex.

Liver
Stomach

Small intestine
Large intestine
Radius (forearm bone)
Ulna (forearm bone)

★

The kidneys are in the middle of the back. They filter waste chemicals from your blood and control the amount of water in the body.

Bladder

Carpals (wrist bones)
Metacarpals (hand bones)
Phalanges (finger bones)

Blood vessels

Artery (carries blood away from the heart)

Vein (carries blood back to the heart)

★

Muscle

Tendon – a type of tough, stringy body tissue that connects muscles to bones.

Look inside

This picture shows how body parts are arranged inside your body. Most of your organs are neatly packed together inside the chest and the abdomen (the part of the body between the chest and the legs). The head also has a few organs, including the brain, eyes and ears. The biggest organ, your skin, covers your whole body.

The rest of your body, including arms and legs, is made up of body tissues – including bones, muscles and fat.

Tibia (lower leg bone)
Fibula (lower leg bone)

Ankle
Foot
Toes

INTERNET LINK

For a link to a website where you can see amazing scans of the inside of the human body, go to www.usborne.com/quicklinks

9

Body systems

Most of your body parts work together in groups called body systems. For example, your digestive system is a set of organs, tubes and body tissues that helps you eat and digest food. You have ten main body systems altogether.

Tangled together

Your body systems are all intertwined with each other. For example, the circulatory system reaches into all the other body systems to take blood to them.

Some body parts belong to more than one system. Your throat, for example, is part of your digestive system and part of your respiratory system, because you use it for both swallowing and breathing.

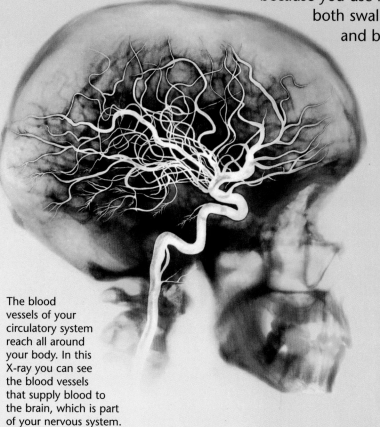

The blood vessels of your circulatory system reach all around your body. In this X-ray you can see the blood vessels that supply blood to the brain, which is part of your nervous system.

INTERNET LINK

For a link to a website where you can find facts, images and a quiz about the main body systems, go to **www.usborne.com/quicklinks**

See the systems

These pictures show your main body systems, each in a separate diagram. In real life, they are all tightly packed together inside your body.

Skeletal system

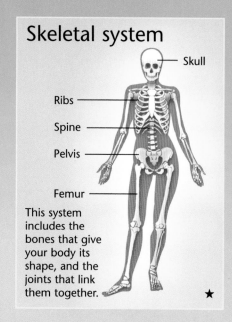

Skull
Ribs
Spine
Pelvis
Femur

This system includes the bones that give your body its shape, and the joints that link them together. ★

Nervous system

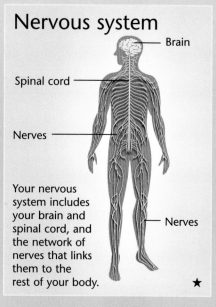

Brain
Spinal cord
Nerves
Nerves

Your nervous system includes your brain and spinal cord, and the network of nerves that links them to the rest of your body. ★

Endocrine system

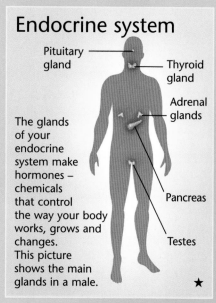

Pituitary gland
Thyroid gland
Adrenal glands
Pancreas
Testes

The glands of your endocrine system make hormones – chemicals that control the way your body works, grows and changes. This picture shows the main glands in a male. ★

Muscular system

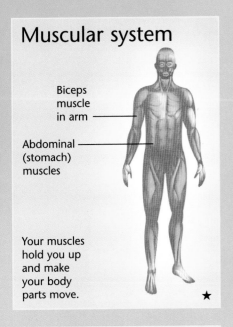

Biceps muscle in arm

Abdominal (stomach) muscles

Your muscles hold you up and make your body parts move.

★

Skin, hair and nails

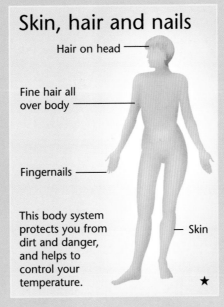

Hair on head

Fine hair all over body

Fingernails

Skin

This body system protects you from dirt and danger, and helps to control your temperature.

★

Digestive system

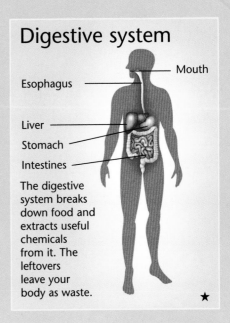

Mouth

Esophagus

Liver

Stomach

Intestines

The digestive system breaks down food and extracts useful chemicals from it. The leftovers leave your body as waste.

★

Respiratory system

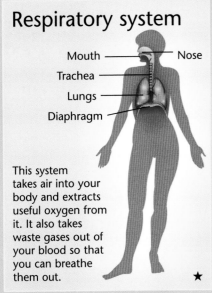

Mouth — Nose

Trachea

Lungs

Diaphragm

This system takes air into your body and extracts useful oxygen from it. It also takes waste gases out of your blood so that you can breathe them out.

★

Circulatory system

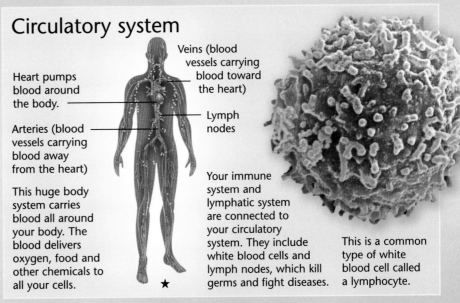

Heart pumps blood around the body.

Arteries (blood vessels carrying blood away from the heart)

Veins (blood vessels carrying blood toward the heart)

Lymph nodes

This huge body system carries blood all around your body. The blood delivers oxygen, food and other chemicals to all your cells.

★

Your immune system and lymphatic system are connected to your circulatory system. They include white blood cells and lymph nodes, which kill germs and fight diseases.

This is a common type of white blood cell called a lymphocyte.

Urinary system

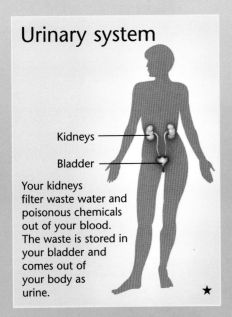

Kidneys

Bladder

Your kidneys filter waste water and poisonous chemicals out of your blood. The waste is stored in your bladder and comes out of your body as urine.

★

Reproductive system

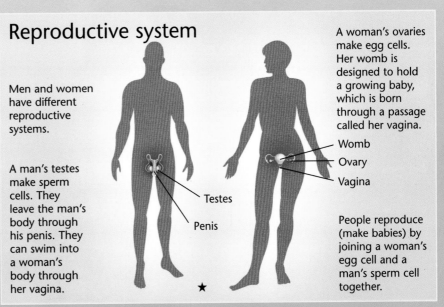

Men and women have different reproductive systems.

A man's testes make sperm cells. They leave the man's body through his penis. They can swim into a woman's body through her vagina.

Testes

Penis

★

A woman's ovaries make egg cells. Her womb is designed to hold a growing baby, which is born through a passage called her vagina.

Womb

Ovary

Vagina

People reproduce (make babies) by joining a woman's egg cell and a man's sperm cell together.

Cells

Your body is made up of cells. Whenever you look at your hand or at a drop of blood, you're looking at millions of cells packed tightly together. But on their own, most cells are too tiny to see. In all, you have 50 trillion to 100 trillion cells in your body.

This is a diatom, a tiny single-celled plant, shown 300 times bigger than in real life. Many living things have only one cell.

INTERNET LINK

For a link to a website where you can find out a lot more about different types of cells, go to **www.usborne.com/quicklinks**

What is a cell?

A cell is a tiny living unit with its own protective "skin." Inside, a cell has several parts, called organelles, which help it to work. The cells that make up your body are working all the time to keep you alive. They make body chemicals, carry messages, and help you to think, move, eat and breathe.

This is a microscope photo of human fat. You can see how it is made up of clusters of round fat cells.

Making proteins

Your cells make chemicals called proteins, which help to make new cells or are used to do different jobs around your body. Proteins are made up of simpler chemicals called amino acids. By combining amino acids in different ways, your cells can make thousands of different kinds of proteins.

Kinds of cells

The human body has over 200 kinds of cells, including muscle cells, blood cells, nerve cells, liver cells, fat cells and skin cells. Different kinds of cells do different jobs. Here are some of them:

★ **Red blood cells** are shaped like flattened balls. They carry oxygen around your body.

Muscle cells are long and thin. They can shorten themselves to make muscles work.

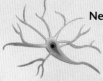

Nerve cells carry messages around your brain and to and from other parts of your body.

Women's **egg cells** are some of the biggest human cells. They are just big enough to see with the naked eye.

Inside a cell

Although body cells can look very different from each other, most of them have the same parts. The skin around a cell is called the cell membrane. Each cell also has a control unit called a nucleus. The cell's other parts, or organelles, float around in a watery jelly called cytoplasm.

This picture shows a typical cell, cut open to reveal its main parts.

Ribosomes are organelles that make new proteins.

This is the **endoplasmic reticulum**. It transports proteins made by the ribosomes to other parts of the cell.

Lysosomes destroy old, damaged organelles and any dangerous substances which get into the cell.

The cell is full of runny **cytoplasm**. It is mostly made of water, with thin strands of protein running through it.

The **cytoskeleton** is made of tiny tubes and threads that help to give the cell its shape.

The **nucleus** controls everything that happens in the cell, using chemical signals. It also contains the instructions for making new cells.

The **Golgi complex** stores proteins made by the ribosomes. It may also prepare the proteins for different uses.

Some cells have finger-like shapes called **cilia** on the outside. They help the cell to move things like food particles toward it.

The **mitochondria** turn food particles and oxygen into energy, so that the cell can keep working.

The **cell membrane** protects the cell and holds it together. It also controls the way substances such as food particles and water pass into and out of the cell.

Inside the nucleus

The cell nucleus controls what happens inside the cell, including the jobs the cell does and the proteins it makes. The nucleus can do this because it contains complicated instructions called genes, which are made of long strands of a chemical called DNA. You can find out more about genes and DNA on the next page.

Making new cells ★

Every second, millions of cells in your body die, and new ones have to be made. Most cells make new cells by dividing into two. But some kinds of cells, such as heart muscle cells, do not keep dying and being replaced. You keep the same ones for your whole life.

These pictures show how a cell divides. First, the cell grows to twice its original size.

The nucleus makes a copy of its DNA and splits into two nuclei.

The enlarged double cell begins to split in two down the middle.

Finally, the two new cells separate from each other.

13

Genes and DNA

The way your body grows, the way it works, and what you look like are all decided by what your cells do. But how do cells know what to do? The answer is genes. They are the instructions inside a cell nucleus that tell the cell how to work.

Cell

Cell wall

Organelles

Cytoplasm

Cell nucleus

What are genes?

Genes are instructions made of strings of chemicals. They tell your cells how to build your body and how to make the substances they need. This means genes control the way your body grows and the way it works from day to day. Everyone has a complete set of human genes, with slight differences that make each person unique. Most of the cells in your body contain a copy of your complete set of genes.

In real life, chromosomes are found inside the cell nucleus. In this diagram, a chromosome has been enlarged and its DNA has been unwound, so that you can see how it works.

Chromosomes (strands of DNA) are stored inside the cell nucleus.

One gene

A **gene** is a section of a chromosome.

There are many genes on each chromosome.

Chromosomes are made of a chemical called DNA.

What is DNA?

DNA is the substance that genes are made of. The letters DNA are short for a chemical called deoxyribonucleic acid. It has a long, thin shape like a twisted ladder. Each cell contains 46 long strands of DNA (23 pairs). Each of these strands is called a chromosome. A gene is a section of DNA that makes up part of a chromosome. Each chromosome has many different genes along it.

DNA is made up of four chemicals known as **bases**, arranged in a spiral ladder shape.

In a gene, the pattern of the four bases acts as a code for a particular body substance.

In this diagram, the four bases are represented by four different colors.

★

How genes work

DNA contains four different chemicals, called bases. In a gene, the bases are arranged in a sequence that acts as a code for a particular body protein (a type of body substance). When a cell needs to make a protein – such as keratin, which is used to make hair – it finds the right gene and reads the code. Then it fits chemicals together in the right order. The chemicals it uses come from food, and are delivered to your cells in your blood.

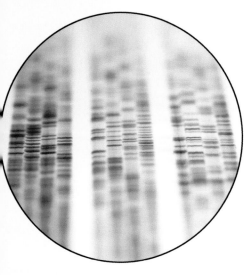

This is a printout of the pattern of bases in a sample of human DNA. Scientists use powerful computers to read DNA patterns.

DNA fingerprinting

Because most people have their own, unique DNA patterns, DNA testing (also called DNA fingerprinting) can be used to identify people. For example, the DNA patterns in blood cells left at a crime scene will only match the DNA of someone who was there. This helps police scientists, called forensic scientists, to identify crime suspects.

Passing on genes

The genes inside your cells are unique to you (unless you're an identical twin, as identical twins have the same genes). Your own special set of genes is made of a mixture of half your mother's genes, and half your father's genes. They came from the cells in your parents' bodies that were used to make you. This is why people often look similar to their parents.

In this family, you can see that both the children look a little like their mother. Each of them has inherited a copy of half of the genes inside her cells, and half of the genes inside their dad's cells.

Dolly the sheep was the first healthy mammal cloned from another adult mammal.

BODY SCIENCE: Cloning

Cloning means making an exact copy of a living thing by copying its DNA. Scientists have worked out how to take the DNA from an animal's cell, and insert it into an egg cell that has had its DNA removed. They then use an electrical signal to make the new cell start growing into a baby animal. Using this method, scientists have cloned several kinds of animals, and may be able to clone humans too.

INTERNET LINK

For a link to a website where you can find out how to make an edible model of a DNA molecule, go to
www.usborne.com/quicklinks

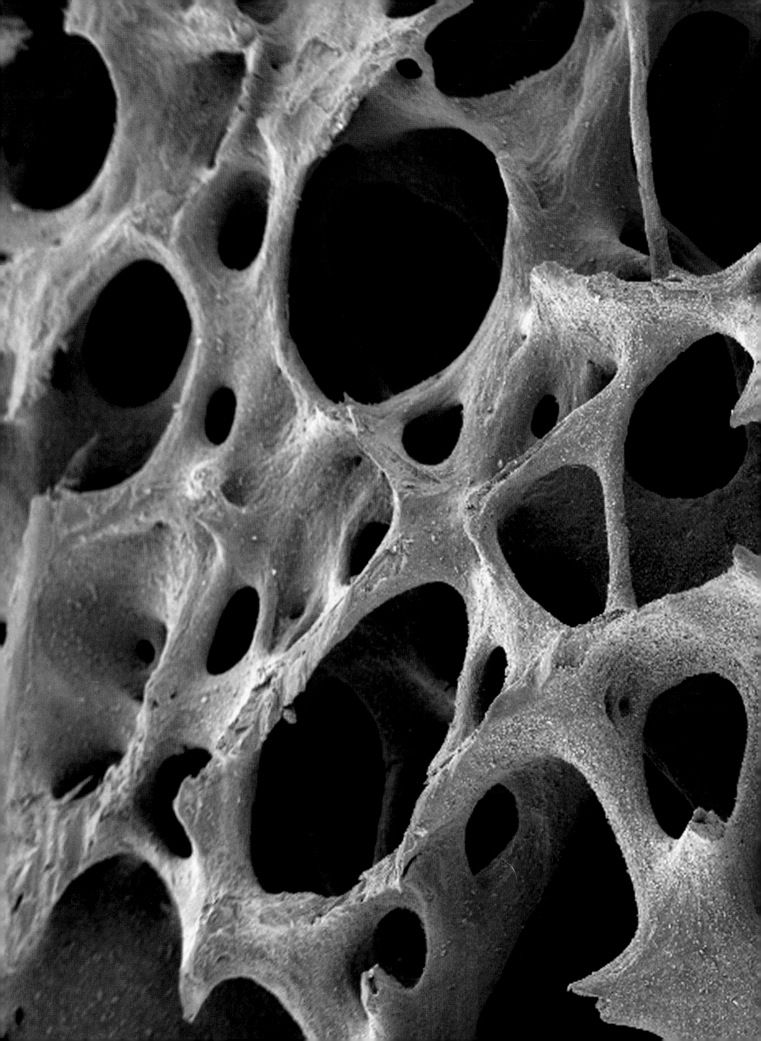

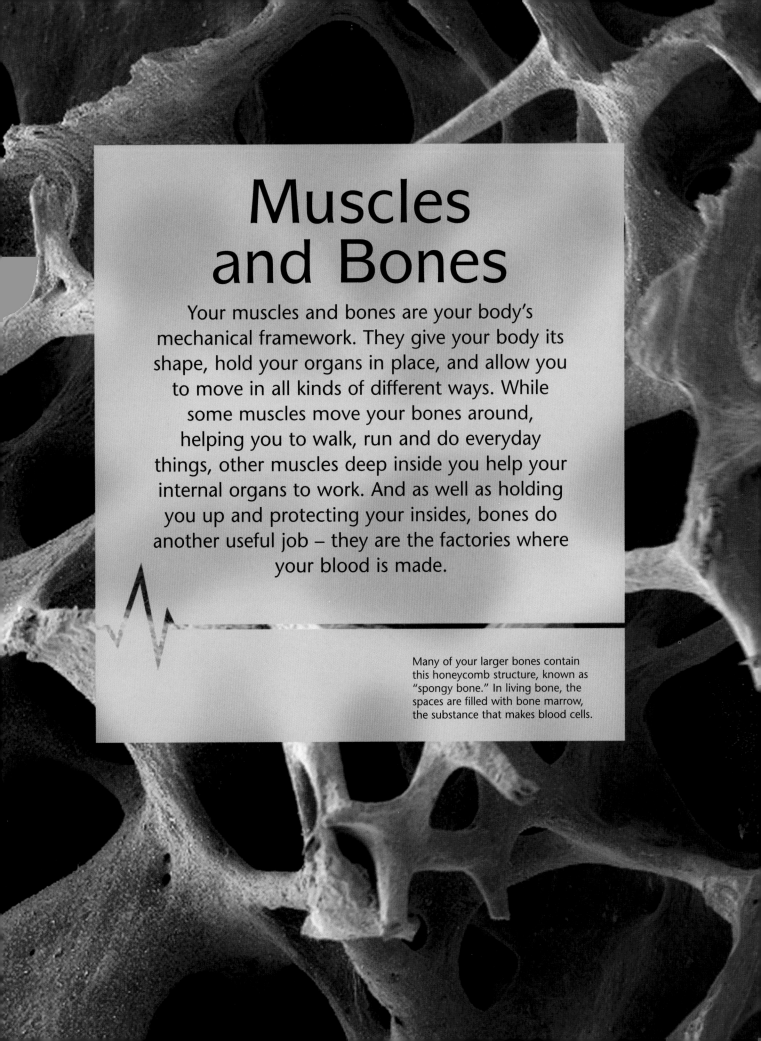

Muscles and Bones

Your muscles and bones are your body's mechanical framework. They give your body its shape, hold your organs in place, and allow you to move in all kinds of different ways. While some muscles move your bones around, helping you to walk, run and do everyday things, other muscles deep inside you help your internal organs to work. And as well as holding you up and protecting your insides, bones do another useful job – they are the factories where your blood is made.

Many of your larger bones contain this honeycomb structure, known as "spongy bone." In living bone, the spaces are filled with bone marrow, the substance that makes blood cells.

The skeleton

Your skeleton holds your body up. Without it, you'd be a shapeless sack of organs, unable to walk or even sit up. Your bones have other jobs too. They make blood, store minerals, and protect important organs, like your brain, from getting squashed.

How many bones?

An adult's body has 206 bones, but children have more. A baby is born with up to 270 bones. Many of them fuse together to make bigger bones as the baby grows older. Almost half of your bones are in your hands and feet, because this is where you need to make the most complex movements.

Your wrist contains a group of small, rounded bones like pebbles, called the carpals.

The large picture on this page is an X-ray of a real human skeleton. It shows clearly how the bones in the skeleton fit together inside the body.

The **stapes**, the smallest bone in the human body, is inside the ear. It's less than ¼in long.

Skull

Clavicle (collarbone)

Scapula (shoulder blade)

Sternum (breastbone)

Ribs form a cage around your heart and lungs, and are used in breathing.

Humerus

Radius

Ulna

Metacarpal

The **vertebral column**, or **spine**, is made up of 33 round bones called vertebrae.

Pelvis

The **coccyx** is at the base of the spine. Scientists think it's the human version of a tail.

The **femur**, or **thighbone**, is the longest bone in the body.

Patella (kneecap)

Tibia

Fibula

Metatarsal

Bone names

All the bones in the skeleton have their own scientific names. They are mostly in Latin, so that doctors and scientists around the world can all use the same names. For example, "patella" (Latin for "dish") is the scientific name for the kneecap.

INTERNET LINK

For a link to a website where you can take a tour of the human skeleton and play an interactive game, go to **www.usborne.com/quicklinks**

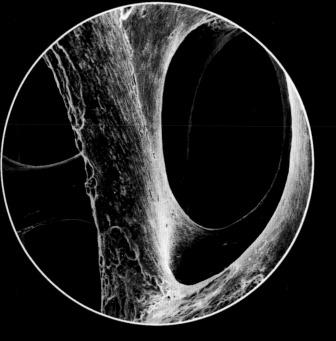

This is a close-up photo of the honeycomb structure inside a bone, at about 70 times life-size.

Bone layers

Bones are made up of several layers. The tough outer layer is called the periosteum. Under that is a layer of solid or "compact" bone, and under that is a lighter, honeycomb layer called "spongy bone" (although it's still hard, not soft and soggy).

Large bones have a soft substance called bone marrow in the middle and among the spongy bone. This is where new blood cells are made. Blood vessels carry the new blood cells out of the bone to wherever the body needs them.

What are bones made of?

Bones are mostly made of hard minerals, including calcium, which comes from foods such as milk, cheese and broccoli. But bones aren't just solid sticks. They contain living cells, and have blood vessels and nerves running through them. That's why it hurts when you break a bone, and why a broken bone can heal and mend itself.

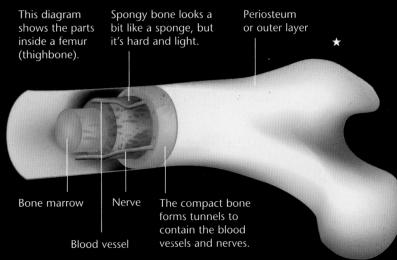

This diagram shows the parts inside a femur (thighbone).

Spongy bone looks a bit like a sponge, but it's hard and light.

Periosteum or outer layer ★

Bone marrow   Nerve   The compact bone forms tunnels to contain the blood vessels and nerves.

Blood vessel

Growing bones

If bones are hard, how do children's bones grow? The answer is that their skeletons aren't all bony. Some of their bones are made of a softer material, called cartilage.

★

A 12-year-old's bones contain cartilage discs. They grow to make bones longer.

By the age of about 20, the cartilage has become bone, and can't grow any more.

By the time a child is 12, most of this cartilage hardens into real bone. But the long bones in your legs and arms still keep growing until you're almost 20. To do this, each bone keeps a small disc of cartilage near each end, which can keep growing.

BODY SCIENCE: Bone detectives

Archaeologists often find the bones of people who died centuries ago. They can reveal a lot about how people used to live. For example, minerals found in bones show what people ate.

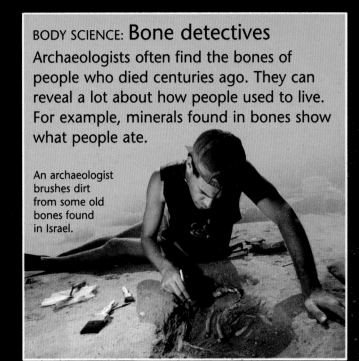

An archaeologist brushes dirt from some old bones found in Israel.

Joints

Wherever two bones meet, there's a joint. There's one at each elbow, knee, shoulder and hip, and dozens in your hands, feet and spine. Joints let your skeleton flex, so that you can move your body around.

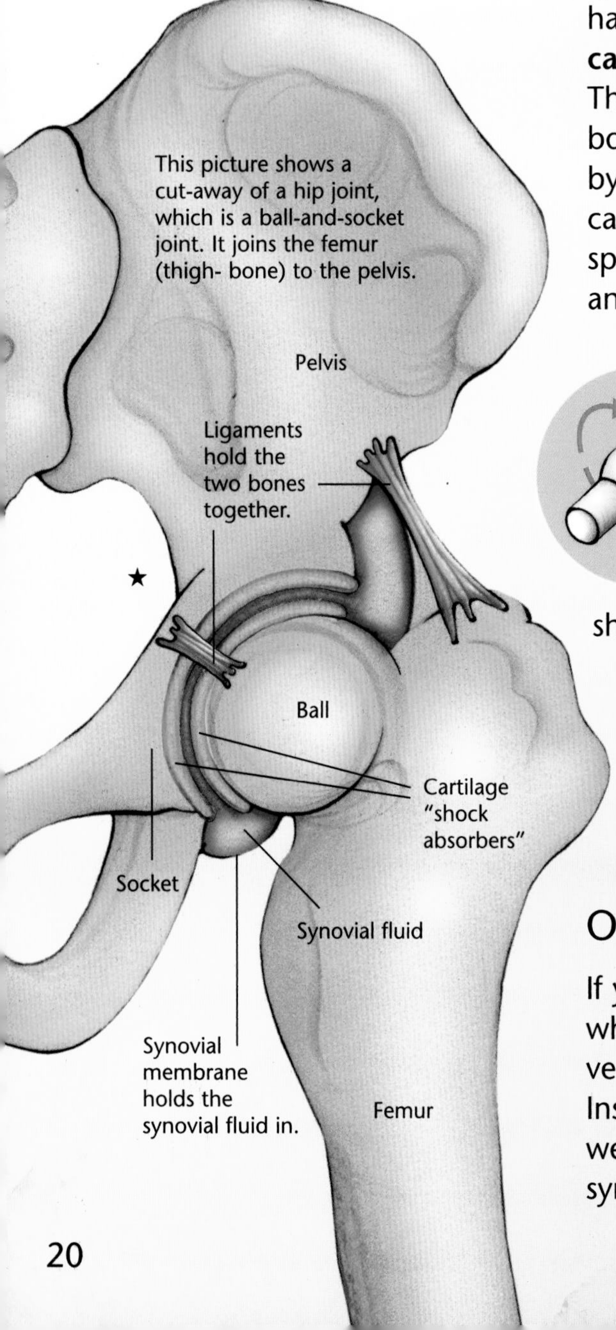

This picture shows a cut-away of a hip joint, which is a ball-and-socket joint. It joins the femur (thigh- bone) to the pelvis.

Pelvis

Ligaments hold the two bones together.

★

Ball

Socket

Cartilage "shock absorbers"

Synovial fluid

Synovial membrane holds the synovial fluid in.

Femur

Types of joints

You have lots of different kinds of joints, allowing your body to move in different ways. Here are some of them:

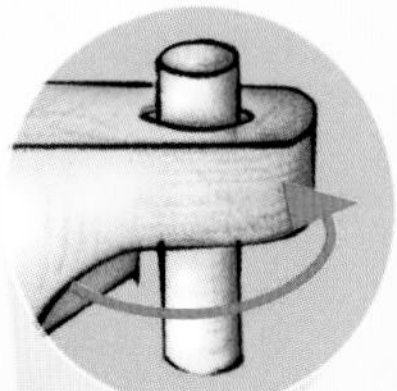

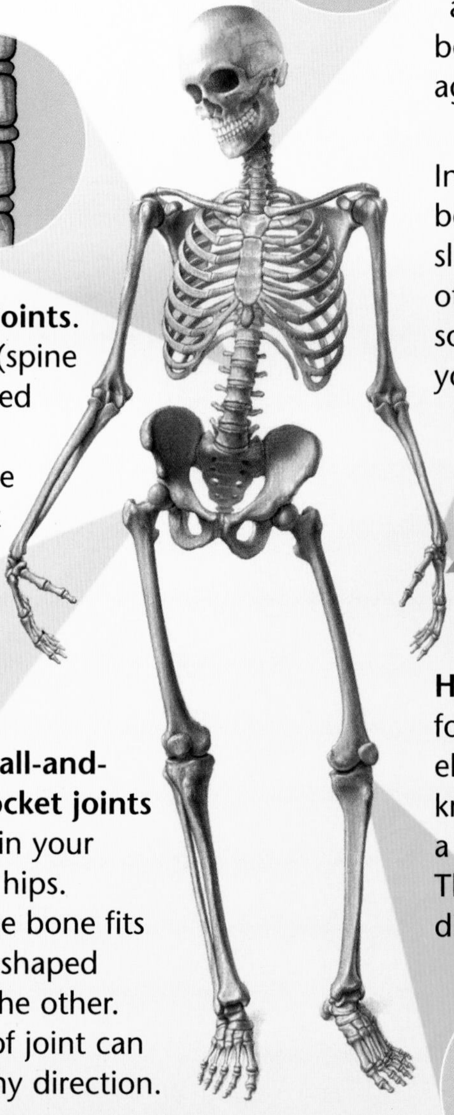

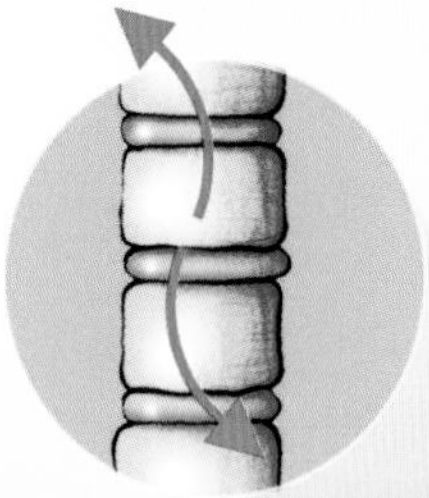

Your spine has many **cartilaginous joints**. The vertebrae (spine bones) are linked by discs of cartilage, so the spine can twist and bend.

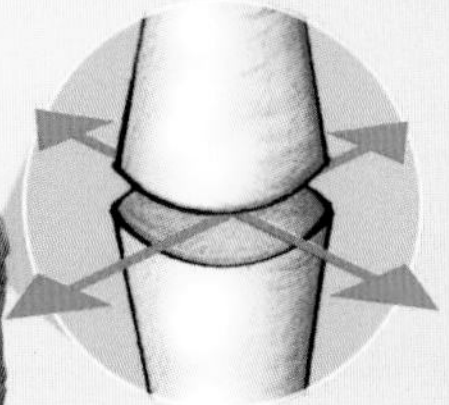

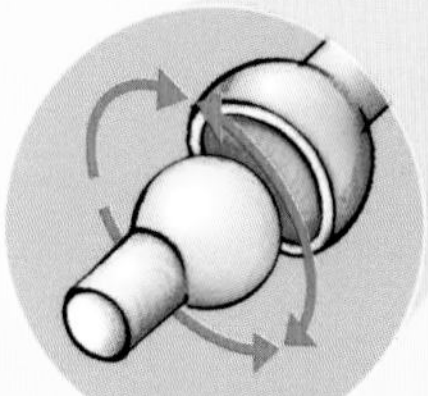

Ball-and-socket joints are in your shoulders and hips. A ball on one bone fits into a cup-shaped socket in the other. This kind of joint can move in any direction.

A **pivot joint**, like the one at the top of your neck, allows one bone to rotate against another.

In **gliding joints**, bones simply slide over each other. There are some of these in your wrists.

Hinged joints, found in fingers, elbows and knees, work like a door hinge. They flex in one direction only.

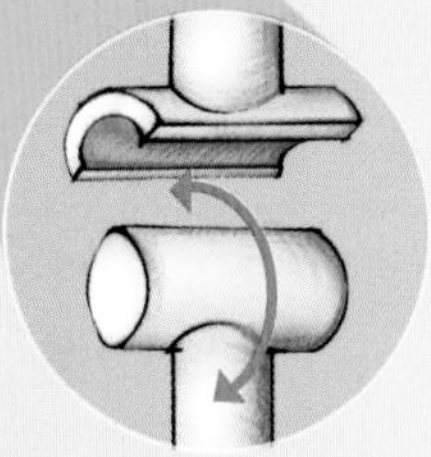

Oil and cushions

If your bones scraped together when you moved, it would be very painful (and creaky). Instead, most joints are kept well-oiled by a liquid called synovial fluid. It's held around the joint in a pocket called the synovial membrane. Bones also have cushions of rubbery cartilage at the ends. They act like shock absorbers when your joints move.

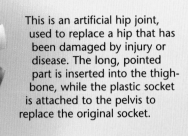

This is an artificial hip joint, used to replace a hip that has been damaged by injury or disease. The long, pointed part is inserted into the thigh-bone, while the plastic socket is attached to the pelvis to replace the original socket.

This is an X-ray picture of a dislocated finger. You can see where the first and second phalanges (finger bones) have been pushed apart.

Out of place

Joints can sometimes be dislocated in an accident. When this happens, the bones in the joint get pushed away from each other and the joint stops working. A dislocated joint hurts a lot, but doctors can usually fix it by pushing it back together.

Ligaments

Ligaments hold together the two bones on either side of a joint, to stop them from falling apart. Ligaments are like very thick, tough elastic bands. A sprain happens when a ligament gets pulled too far and is damaged.

This photo shows how the dislocated finger looks from the outside. It may be possible to push the bones back into position without the need for an operation.

Double-jointed people don't really have double joints. They just have extra-long, stretchy ligaments, which allow their joints to move farther than most peoples'.

INTERNET LINK

For a link to a website where you can answer quiz questions and watch a movie about joints, go to www.usborne.com/quicklinks

Are you supple?

If you're supple, it means your ligaments are stretchy and your joints are very flexible. Being very supple means you can bend your body into lots of positions, such as touching your toes, doing the splits or putting your foot behind your ear. Some people are naturally more supple than others, but you can make your joints more flexible by doing exercises such as yoga to stretch your ligaments.

A contortionist is someone who can move their body into unusual positions. This contortionist is performing in the street in Shanghai, China.

21

Muscles and tendons

Your bones and joints are arranged so that they can move – but not by themselves. They need muscles. Muscles lie next to bones and pull them into different positions, so that you can walk, run, kick a ball or peel a banana.

Skeletal muscles

The muscles you use to move around are called skeletal muscles, because they're mostly attached to your skeleton. You have over 600 of them altogether, and they make up nearly half of your total body weight. Each muscle is a red, stretchy bundle that can contract (get shorter) and relax again. It is this contracting movement which makes muscles pull on your bones to make you move.

Muscles in pairs

Muscles can only pull – they can't push. So muscles often have to work in pairs to make body parts move. For example, you use one muscle to bend your arm, and another to pull it straight again.

This picture shows how skeletal muscles are wrapped around your bones, covering them up. Like bones, most muscles have Latin names which scientists around the world can understand.

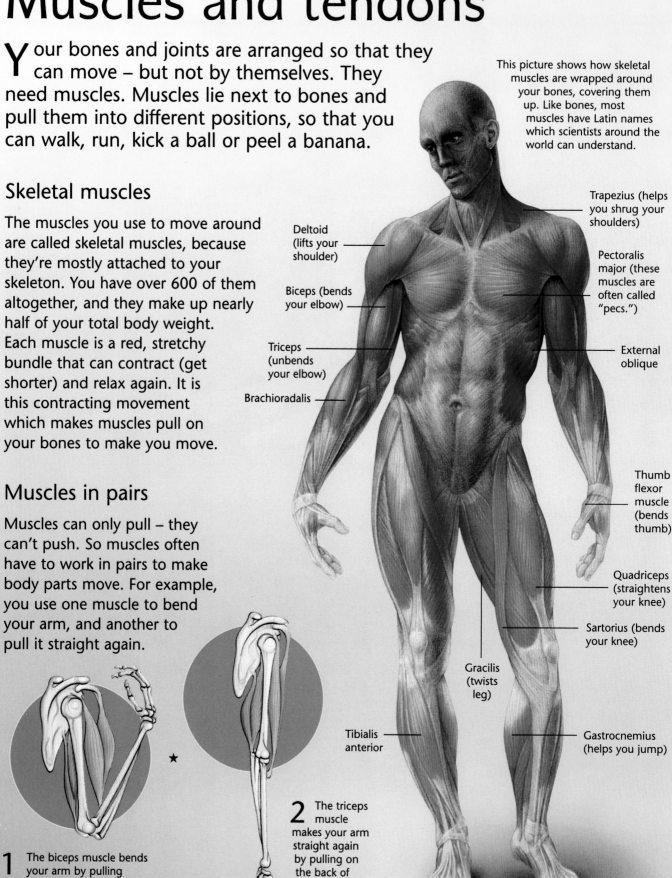

Deltoid (lifts your shoulder)

Biceps (bends your elbow)

Triceps (unbends your elbow)

Brachioradalis

Trapezius (helps you shrug your shoulders)

Pectoralis major (these muscles are often called "pecs.")

External oblique

Thumb flexor muscle (bends thumb)

Quadriceps (straightens your knee)

Sartorius (bends your knee)

Gracilis (twists leg)

Tibialis anterior

Gastrocnemius (helps you jump)

★

1 The biceps muscle bends your arm by pulling your forearm bones upward.

2 The triceps muscle makes your arm straight again by pulling on the back of your elbow.

Muscle fuel

Just like cars and electric drills, muscles need a supply of fuel to give them the energy they need to work. Muscle fuel is a mixture of the food you eat and the oxygen you breathe in.

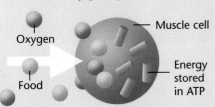

Oxygen

Food

Muscle cell

Energy stored in ATP

Inside your muscle cells, oxygen and food are combined to make energy.

Energy is stored in your muscles in a chemical called ATP (adenosine triphosphate), ready for when you need it.

Why muscles ache

When you use your muscles a lot, for example to run a race, the energy in your ATP gets used up. Your muscles need more oxygen, so you breathe faster to take in as much air as possible. But if the oxygen doesn't reach your muscles fast enough, they try to make energy without it. This works for a while, but not very well. It releases a poison called lactic acid into your muscles, making them hurt. This tells your body to stop and rest until you have recovered.

BODY SCIENCE:
Muscles in space

When astronauts come back to Earth after a long trip in space, they find it hard to walk, because they have been in zero gravity. On Earth, muscles have to work against gravity to hold you up. Without gravity, they get weaker and weaker.

In space, astronauts can float around freely. Their muscles do not get the daily exercise of fighting against gravity.

Sprinters push their muscles to the limit when they run. After a race, a sprinter is exhausted and has to rest so that the oxygen his or her muscle cells have used up can be replaced.

Tugging tendons

The end of each muscle narrows into a tough cord called a tendon, which is attached to a bone. When the muscle contracts, the tendon pulls on the bone.

This diagram shows the complicated network of tendons inside your hand. They are attached to muscles in your arm.

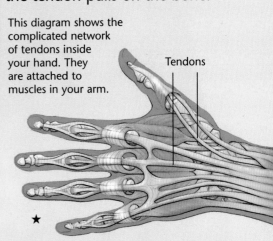

Tendons

★

You can feel one of the biggest tendons in the body, the Achilles tendon, just above your heel. It feels hard like a bone, but if you press it, it will bend slightly. This tendon joins strong muscles in your calf to the bone in your heel. It's used to pull up your heel when you walk or run.

23

How muscles work

Every time you decide to make a movement, like scratching your nose or touching the screen on your phone, there's a complicated chain of events inside your body. Your brain, nerves and muscles all have to work together to make the movement happen. But they do it so fast, you hardly notice.

This microscope photo shows muscle fibers (red) and nerve endings pressing against them (green).

Message to move

When you want to move, your brain sends a message to your muscles. Electrical and chemical signals travel down your spinal cord, then branch off along nerves leading to your muscles. At the ends, your nerves divide into thousands of nerve endings. Each muscle cell has a nerve ending touching it. The signal travels through the nerve endings and onto the muscle cells, telling them to act.

INTERNET LINK

For a link to a website where you can find out more about how muscles work, go to
www.usborne.com/quicklinks

This diagram shows the parts of a muscle. Each muscle contains many tiny, string-like muscle cells, which contract to make the whole muscle contract.

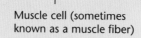

Muscle cell (sometimes known as a muscle fiber)

Actin filament

Myosin filament

Muscles under the microscope

But how do muscle cells actually get shorter? Each muscle cell contains two different kinds of thin strands or filaments, which overlap each other. When they receive the signal to contract, they lock into each other and pull closer together, making the muscle cell shorter, and so making the muscle contract.

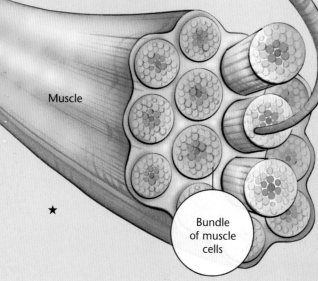

Muscle

★

Bundle of muscle cells

This is what happens inside a muscle fiber when your muscle contracts.

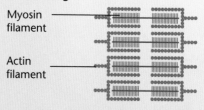

Contracting

Myosin filament

Actin filament

Relaxing   ★

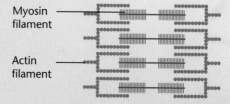

Myosin filament

Actin filament

Amazing muscles

The biggest muscles in the body are the gluteus maximus muscles in your buttocks. But the one that can exert the most force is the jaw muscle, or masseter. It's quite small, but it can make your jaws press together very hard. The pressure of a normal person's bite can be up to 200 pounds – the same as the weight of a fully grown man.

The masseter muscles are at the sides of the face. They pull your upper and lower jaws together.

★   Masseter muscle

Body building

It's possible to build up muscles and make them stronger by doing exercises. When you exercise, your body gradually makes your muscle cells thicker and stronger, and your muscles grow bigger. This usually happens about a day after the exercise, not immediately.

A 19th-century illustration showing a strongman lifting six people at once. Strongmen and bodybuilders increase their strength using special exercises.

The muscles in our faces allow us to communicate all kinds of thoughts and feelings, such as fear, anger or playfulness.

Making faces

Muscles aren't just for strength and getting around. They are also important because they allow us to communicate with each other. Your face has about 80 small, precise muscles for moving your mouth and tongue into different shapes to make words, and for making different facial expressions. For example, when you grin, you're using about 17 different face muscles. A frown uses even more muscles – about 43.

Moving without thinking

You don't have to remember to squeeze food along your intestines or make your heart beat all day long, but these things still happen. They are done by your involuntary muscles.

Smooth muscle

Involuntary muscles are made from a kind of muscle called smooth muscle. Instead of being attached to your bones, smooth muscle is found in organs such as the eyes and stomach. It helps them to work without you even thinking about them.

Part of your brain is always hard at work keeping control of your smooth muscles and checking that they're working properly. But this isn't the part you use for thinking, so it doesn't feel as if you're using your brain at all.

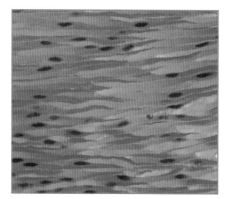

This picture shows human smooth muscle under a microscope. Instead of being striped like skeletal muscle, it's made up of bundles of long cells with pointed ends.

Squeezing along

Smooth muscles are found in many of the tubes, such as intestines, that carry food and liquid around inside your body. They are arranged in ring shapes, and work by squeezing to push food or liquid along. This pushing effect is called peristalsis.

Gall bladder

Bile from the gall bladder goes into this tube, called the cystic duct.

Rings of smooth muscle in the cystic duct squeeze tightly to push the bile along.

Bile

Your gall bladder makes a liquid called bile that helps you digest food. This diagram shows how smooth muscles move the bile to your intestines.

★

Gradually the bile is squeezed all the way to your small intestine.

Hardworking heart

The heart is made of a special kind of involuntary muscle called cardiac muscle. It's the hardest-working muscle in your body. It works non-stop, squeezing and relaxing about 100,000 times a day to pump blood around your body. It never gets tired out or needs a rest.

You can sometimes feel your heart muscle beating (pumping) if you put your hand near the top of your chest. It beats faster when you exercise, because your muscles need extra blood so that they can work harder. Your heart can also beat faster if you're scared or excited.

In this computer-generated image of a pumping heart, the heart muscle is shown in blue.

INTERNET LINK

For links to two websites where you can see animations showing peristalsis and the heart beating, go to **www.usborne.com/quicklinks**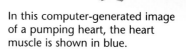

Letting in light

The iris, the colored part of the eye around the pupil, is a smooth muscle. If you try making your pupil bigger and smaller by thinking about it, you can't do it. But your brain can tell the iris to contract or relax, depending on how much light there is.

To see this working, look in a mirror in a dimly lit room. Your pupil will be quite large. Then ask someone to switch the light on while you watch. The iris will shrink your pupil, so that it doesn't let in too much light.

Your pupil is the black hole that lets light into your eye. The iris (the colored part) is a smooth muscle that surrounds it and controls its size.

Breathing

Breathing is an unusual kind of involuntary movement. Normally, you breathe without thinking. Your brain unconsciously controls a set of muscles that make your chest expand, sucking air into your lungs. When these muscles relax, your chest shrinks and you breathe out.

However, you can control your breathing if you want to. This is very useful. It lets you do things like play the trumpet, blow out a candle or hold your breath underwater.

These pictures show how muscles in your chest make you breathe.

Breathing in

Lungs

Rib muscles

Diaphragm

To breathe in, muscles attached to your ribs pull your chest out and up, and your diaphragm moves down. This makes your lungs expand, and air is sucked in.

Breathing out

Lungs

Rib muscles

Diaphragm ★

To breathe out, your diaphragm pushes upward and your rib muscles squeeze your ribs together. Your lungs shrink and push air out.

To play a wind instrument, you have to be able to control your breathing carefully.

Reflexes

Reflexes make you do things like pull away from pain, or shut your eyes when you see a bright light. You move before you even have a chance to think about it. This can save vital time when you're in a dangerous situation.

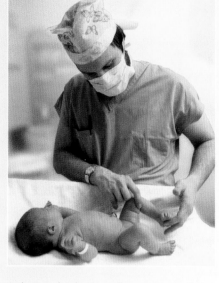

A doctor checks the reflexes of a newborn baby to make sure it is healthy.

Reflex responses

Have you ever touched a hot surface and pulled your hand away before you even felt the pain? That's a reflex response. Your nerves feel the heat and send a message to your spinal cord. It sends a message to pull your hand away at once.

At the same time, a pain message is sent to your brain, but it takes a bit longer to get there. By the time you realize your fingers are burning, you've already taken action.

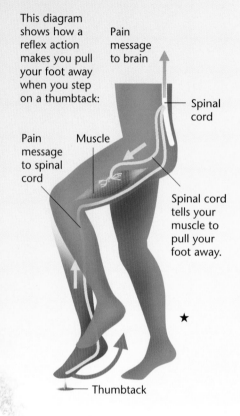

This diagram shows how a reflex action makes you pull your foot away when you step on a thumbtack:

Pain message to brain

Spinal cord

Pain message to spinal cord

Muscle

Spinal cord tells your muscle to pull your foot away.

Thumbtack

The blink reflex makes you close your eyes when something is thrown in your face.

Danger alert

Your reflex responses are always on the alert to keep you out of danger. You blink to protect your eyes if something comes near your face, or if you see a bright light. You sneeze if your nose is irritated by dust, and jump if you hear a loud bang. These things are all signs that your nerves are in good working order. Doctors sometimes test reflexes to make sure there's nothing wrong with your nervous system.

Skin, Hair and Nails

You need skin to hold all your insides together and keep dirt and germs out of your body. Skin also helps to stop your body from getting too dry, too wet, too hot or too cold – and if it's damaged, it can repair itself.

Hair and nails may not look like skin, but they're made of the same substance – a protein called keratin. They too help to protect your body.

A magnified image of human skin, covered with drops of sweat

What is skin?

Skin isn't just the outside of your body. It's an organ, just like your brain and heart. In fact, it's the biggest of all your organs, and it has several vital jobs to do. It protects your insides, feels things, and keeps you at the right temperature.

Skin cells

Skin cells are mostly made of a tough protein called keratin. They are constantly moving up from the deeper layers of your skin to the surface, where they form a flaky, dead layer. About 40 million dead skin cells fall off you each day, to be replaced by new cells from underneath.

The surface of human skin, magnified to hundreds of times life-size

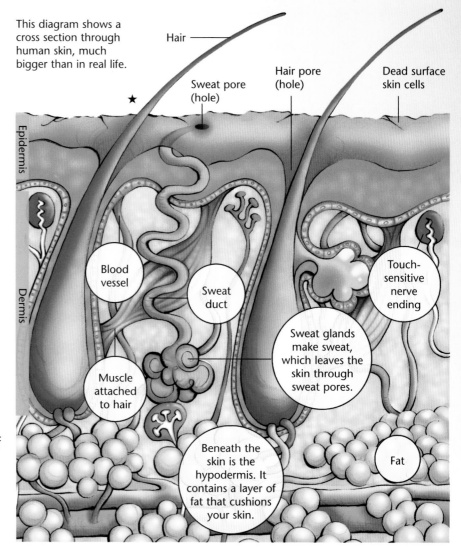

This diagram shows a cross section through human skin, much bigger than in real life.

Hair

Sweat pore (hole)

Hair pore (hole)

Dead surface skin cells

Epidermis

Dermis

Blood vessel

Sweat duct

Touch-sensitive nerve ending

Sweat glands make sweat, which leaves the skin through sweat pores.

Muscle attached to hair

Beneath the skin is the hypodermis. It contains a layer of fat that cushions your skin.

Fat

Under the skin

Skin has two main layers. The top layer, the epidermis, is the skin you can see on your body surface. The lower layer, or dermis, is thicker and contains blood vessels and sweat glands.

Skin sensations

Skin keeps you in touch with the outside world. It's full of tiny receptors that can tell whether you're cool or warm, or touching something soft, hard, rough or smooth. Each receptor is attached to a nerve that sends signals to your brain about what you can feel.

How big?

If you spread out an average adult's skin, it would take up about 2.2 square yards – about as much space as a single bed. It would be heavy too, because skin makes up eight to ten percent of your whole body weight. For an average man, that's around 15 pounds – as heavy as three thick winter coats.

Why don't you soak up water like a sponge when you go swimming? It's because skin is waterproof.

Holding it all in

Your skin acts as a strong, stretchy bag for your muscles, bones, organs and other body parts. It holds everything together and stops dirt and diseases from getting in. Skin is waterproof too. It keeps water out, so you don't turn into a human sponge when it rains. It also holds moisture inside your body, so you don't dry out.

GOING WRONG: Zits

A zit, or pimple, happens when your skin makes too much sebum (oil), which blocks up a hair pore. Dirt, oil and bacteria collect underneath, making a swelling which appears as a sore, red bump.

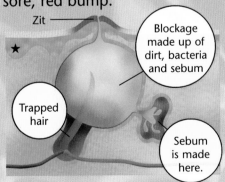

Zit

★

Blockage made up of dirt, bacteria and sebum

Trapped hair

Sebum is made here.

Teenagers often have zits because hormones (chemicals in their bodies) make their skin produce extra sebum.

INTERNET LINK

For a link to a website where you can play games and find out more facts to do with skin, go to **www.usborne.com/quicklinks**

Fingerprints

Under a magnifying glass, you can see the unique patterns and swirls in a fingerprint.

The skin on the tips of your toes and fingers grows in patterns of tiny ridges that help you grip things. When you touch a hard surface, these patterns leave a fingerprint – a mark made of grease and sweat from your skin. No two people have the same patterns. That's why fingerprints are used to track down criminals.

Skin changes

Your skin changes a lot. You might have seen it soaked with sweat when you're hot, covered in goosebumps when you're cold, or tanning after being in the sun. Or you might have had a big scab that's now gone away. These are all part of the skin's job of reacting to the outside world and keeping you safe.

Staying the same

Your body likes to stay at the same temperature – around 98.5°F. Just a few degrees hotter or colder than that, and you could be in danger! Yet you can play sports on a boiling hot day, or go sledding in the snow, without coming to any harm. That's partly because your skin's working all the time to keep you at a healthy temperature.

Warming up

When you're cold, your skin makes goosebumps.

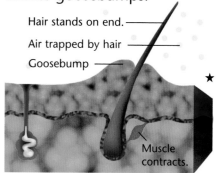

Hair stands on end.
Air trapped by hair
Goosebump
Muscle contracts.

Each hair root is linked to the skin surface by a tiny muscle. In the cold, this muscle contracts, pulling your hair upright and making a bump. The upright hairs help you keep warm by trapping warm air near your skin.

Cooling down

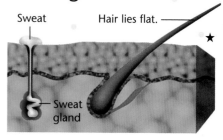

Sweat
Hair lies flat.
Sweat gland

When it's warm, the hairs relax and lie flat, and your skin releases drops of sweat.

You have around three million sweat glands in your skin. When you feel hot, they release drops of sweat that make your skin wet. The sweat turns into water vapor and escapes into the air. To do this, it uses up energy and takes heat from your skin, so you cool down.

If part of your skin (such as your face) is left bare, your body can keep it warm by sending more blood to the surface. That's why people get rosy cheeks when it's cold.

GOING WRONG: Sore and itchy

Some people have skin allergies. They may get a sore, itchy rash if they touch the thing they're allergic to – which could be cat hair, metal objects such as earrings, or strong detergent. If you're allergic to something, there's usually no cure. You just have to stay away from the thing that gives you a rash.

Growing skin

Have you ever run out of skin? Probably not, because skin gets bigger whenever you need it to. As you get taller, put on weight or grow bigger muscles, your skin expands to keep you covered. Even when you grow very fast, your skin keeps up. For example, when a woman is pregnant, she grows a big tummy. Her skin expands to cover the bump. Then, after the baby is born, it shrinks again.

This is a piece of skin grown in a lab. Scientists can take a few skin cells and grow them quickly into sheets of new skin. It can be used to repair skin injuries such as burns.

INTERNET LINK

For a link to a website where you can find out more about sunburn and suntans, go to **www.usborne.com/quicklinks**

Scabs and scars

Skin sometimes gets cut or scraped by accident. When this happens, blood cells join together in a clot to stop you from bleeding. The clot hardens into a scab to cover the wound and keep germs out. Underneath, the skin repairs itself. Finally the scab falls off, leaving just a scar.

This microscope picture shows blood cells forming a clot. They are held together by a thread-like substance called fibrin.

Skin and sun

Your skin uses sunlight to make vitamin D, which keeps bones healthy. But staying in the sun too long can damage skin. If you're in the sun a lot, your skin makes extra supplies of a dark chemical called melanin, which protects you from the sun's rays. This makes lighter types of skin get darker, or tan, in the sun.

These are thermal imaging pictures of a man sunbathing. The hottest areas appear red, and the coldest appear blue. You can see how the man's skin heats up as he lies in the sun.

If you have dark skin, it means you already have lots of melanin and sun protection. But however much you have, it can't protect your skin completely. Too much sun can lead to sunburn, and can even cause skin cancer.

Hair and nails

Hair, fingernails and toenails are made out of keratin, a tough protein which is also found in skin. Like the outer layer of your skin, your hair and nails are mostly dead. They have no nerves, and they're the only parts of the body people regularly cut off. For some people, the way their hair and nails look is an important part of their personality.

This picture shows human head hairs 100 times bigger than life-size. Some of them have "split ends," caused by hairs fraying as they grow.

Hair everywhere

Hair grows almost everywhere on your body. There are only a few non-hairy places, including your lips, the palms of your hands and the soles of your feet.

The hair on your head is the thickest, so it's easy to see. You can probably also spot fine hairs on your forearms. But you'll need a magnifying glass to see the tiny hairs on your knuckles and on the tip of your nose.

How hair grows

Each hair grows out of a hair follicle, which is like a tiny tube in your skin. The follicle contains a hair root made of keratin cells. As the follicle makes more hair cells, the hair is pushed up and out.

This cutaway diagram shows a strand of hair and the skin around it.

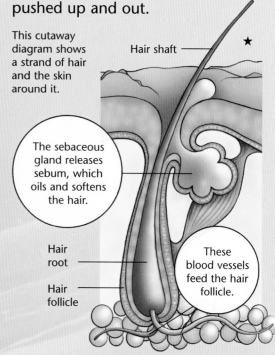

Hair shaft ★

The sebaceous gland releases sebum, which oils and softens the hair.

Hair root

Hair follicle

These blood vessels feed the hair follicle.

The average human body has around five million hair follicles. Every day, hundreds of hairs fall out, and have to start growing again. Each follicle has a six-month rest every few years.

This is a magnified picture of a slice of skin from a human scalp. The dark circles are hair follicles.

Cross section of a hair follicle

INTERNET LINK

For a link to a website where you can find out lots more about hair and nails, go to www.usborne.com/quicklinks

34

Healthy, shiny hair

"Healthy" hair grows from healthy follicles. They use protein and minerals from your bloodstream to make hair. Eating healthy foods, like vegetables and fish, makes your hair grow thick and shiny. Hair conditioner can also make hair shine. It works by smoothing down tiny scales, called cuticles, on the hair's surface.

The cross sections of different types of hair are different shapes:

Curly or frizzy hair is flat or kidney-shaped in cross section.

Straight hair has a round cross section.

Wavy hair is oval in cross section.

Nails

Nails are the human version of claws. Unlike tigers and other wild animals, we don't need claws to catch food, but nails are still very useful. They protect the ends of your fingers and toes from knocks. They also make handy tools. If you had no nails, how would you scratch an itch, open an envelope, peel off a sticker or undo a knot?

Hair, nails and beauty

The ancient Egyptians were dying their hair and painting their nails over 4,000 years ago, and hair and nails have been an important part of human appearance ever since. In most cultures, shiny hair is a sign of youth and beauty. Billions of products for washing, dying, curling and shining hair, and decorating fingernails and toenails, are sold every year.

Most people trim their nails to keep them short. But if they're not trimmed, nails keep growing. This picture shows the fingernails which belonged to Shridhar Chillal of India.

How nails grow

The part of a nail you can see is dead, but each of your nails grows out of a living nail bed. The nail bed is under and behind the nail. At the bottom of each nail, under your skin, is the nail root, where layers of keratin are formed and pushed out toward your fingertips.

Fingernails grow slowly – around 0.1in a month. Toenails are even slower. Both types of nails grow faster in hot weather.

This cutaway diagram of a finger shows the main parts of a fingernail.

The cuticle is a flap of skin protecting the bottom of the nail.

Fingernail

Fingertip

The lunula is a crescent-shaped area of pale skin under the bottom of the nail.

Nail root

Finger bone

The nail bed is under your nail. Nails look pink because of blood vessels in the nail bed.

★

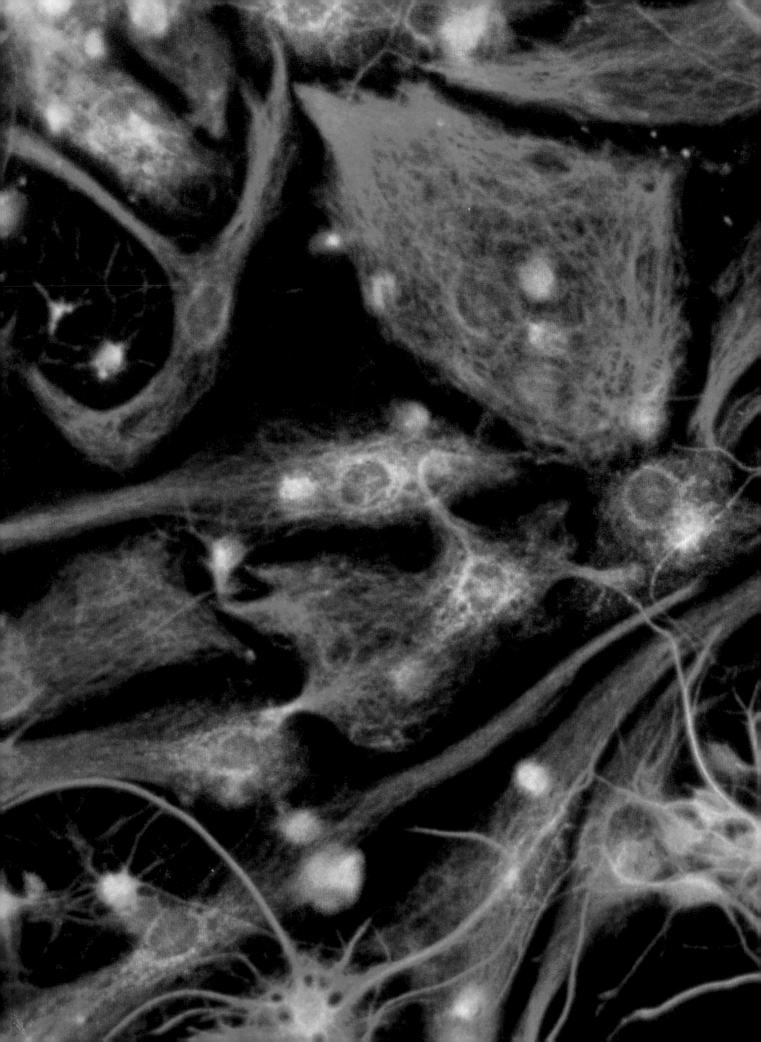

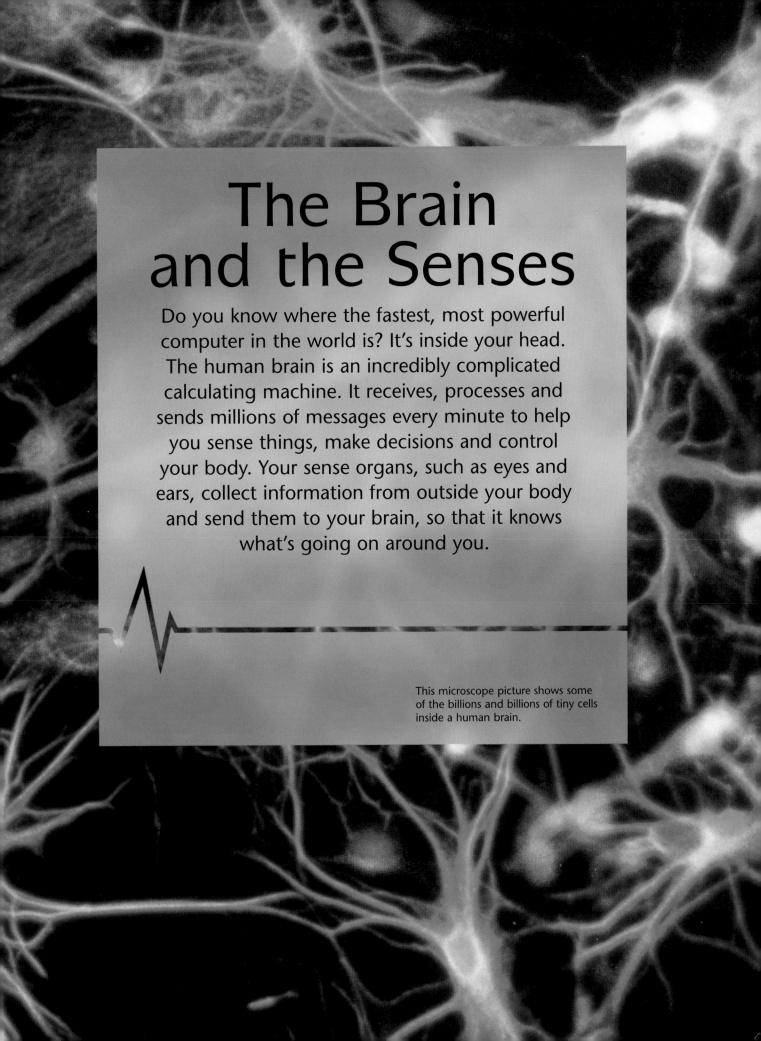

The Brain and the Senses

Do you know where the fastest, most powerful computer in the world is? It's inside your head. The human brain is an incredibly complicated calculating machine. It receives, processes and sends millions of messages every minute to help you sense things, make decisions and control your body. Your sense organs, such as eyes and ears, collect information from outside your body and send them to your brain, so that it knows what's going on around you.

This microscope picture shows some of the billions and billions of tiny cells inside a human brain.

Your amazing brain

Your brain is your body's boss. It controls your movements, thoughts and feelings. It even controls all the things you don't think about, like digesting food and breathing while you're asleep. Your brain also contains your mind – the thing that makes you who you really are.

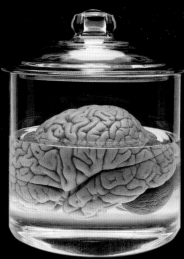

This is a real human brain, preserved to stop it from decaying.

Parts of the brain

Your brain is made up of several parts, which have different jobs to do. This picture shows the main brain parts.

The **cerebrum** is the biggest brain part. It has a wrinkled surface like a walnut, and is split into two halves, or "cerebral hemispheres."

The **cranium** is the part of the skull that surrounds the brain.

The **cortex** is the outer layer of the cerebrum.

The **corpus callosum** is a bundle of fibers joining the two sides of the cerebrum together.

The **thalamus** is in the middle of your brain. It receives signals from your senses and sends them to the correct parts of your brain to be processed.

The **hypothalamus** helps to control body functions such as falling asleep, waking up, sweating and feeling hungry.

The **amygdala** helps you spot danger and feel fear and anxiety.

The **cerebellum** is the second-biggest brain part, and has its own cortex. It helps you keep your balance and control your movements.

The **pituitary gland** makes many hormones, or body chemicals, including growth hormones, which make your body grow as you get older.

The **hippocampus** helps you turn experiences into memories. It also filters out things you don't need to remember.

The **brain stem** joins your brain to your spinal cord and passes messages between your brain and your body. It also controls basic body functions such as heartbeat and digestion.

INTERNET LINK

For a link to a website where you can take a 3-D tour of the amazing brain, go to **www.usborne.com/quicklinks**

Brain sides

Scientists have found that the left half, or hemisphere, of your brain controls the right-hand side of your body, and the right hemisphere controls the left-hand side of your body. Why? Nobody knows.

In this scan of a healthy brain, you can see the hemispheres clearly.

Right eyeball

Right hemisphere

Left eyeball

Left hemisphere

Scientists think the brain's left hemisphere is used more for language and math problems, while the right hemisphere deals more with things like music and pictures. The corpus callosum links them together so that each side knows what the other is doing.

This cross section of a piece of brain is actual size. You can see how the cortex forms the thin outer layer of the brain. In most places it's about 0.1in thick.

The clever cortex

The cortex, the outer layer of the cerebrum, is what you use for thinking. It's very wrinkled, but if it were unfolded and spread out flat, it would be as big as a newspaper. Different parts of the cortex are used for different types of thoughts.

Computer brain

Your brain is more powerful and complicated than the world's biggest computer. It stores millions of memories and does billions of calculations every day. It can also do several jobs, such as seeing, thinking and controlling your movements, all at the same time.

Off with his head!

Long ago, when criminals were often executed by beheading, a French doctor named Dr. Beaurieux did some experiments on severed heads. He claimed they could still see and hear for a few seconds after being chopped off. It took up to 25 seconds for the brain to run out of oxygen and lose consciousness.

The French revolutionary leader Robespierre being beheaded by guillotine in 1794

How the brain works

The brain is amazingly complicated. In fact, it's so complicated that even top brain scientists don't know exactly how it works. However, they do know that nerve cells use electricity and chemicals to send messages zooming around your brain, and to and from your body.

A system of nerves

Your brain is part of a vital body system called the nervous system. Connectors called nerves link your brain to every part of your body. This lets your brain find out what's happening around you, and send instructions to your body to tell it what to do.

The whole nervous system is made up of nerve cells. They are usually known as neurons or neurones.

The nervous system is made up of nerves that reach all around your body. Signals constantly travel along them to and from your brain.

The brain and spinal cord are shown in yellow. They are known as the central nervous system.

The network of nerves reaching to the rest of your body is shown in blue. ★

Neurons

There are three main types of neurons in your nervous system:

Sensory neurons collect information from your sense organs, and carry it to your brain.

From body...   ...to brain

Motor neurons carry instructions from your brain to your muscles, telling them to do things, such as picking up a coin.

From brain...   ...to body

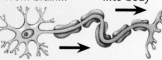

Connector neurons are in your brain and spinal cord. They process information and pass it around to each other.

This large diagram shows a connector neuron in your brain. It's really too tiny to see.

The cell body is the main part of the neuron.

This is the nucleus, the neuron's control unit.

Dendrites are like tentacles reaching out from the cell body. They receive messages from other neurons.

★

Most of the axon is protected by this thick covering, called a myelin sheath.

At the end, the axon splits into branches which pass signals on to the dendrites of other neurons.

The axon is a long tube stretching from one end of the neuron to the other.

Speedy signals

Signals zoom around your nervous system very fast. You can see a coin, decide you want it, and pick it up within a second, yet this involves signals passing through millions of neurons. How do they send such speedy messages? In this picture, you can see how signals jump from one neuron to the next.

1 Messages travel along neurons in the form of electricity. This happens almost instantly.

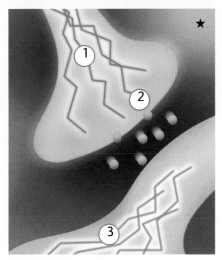

2 The signal travels to the tip of the axon branch. The axon then releases a chemical (shown here as green dots).

3 The chemical jumps across a tiny gap to the dendrite of another neuron, which picks up the signal.

INTERNET LINK

For a link to a website where you can find lots more amazing facts about the brain, go to **www.usborne.com/quicklinks**

Brain tangle

Inside your brain, billions and billions of connector neurons are linked together in a complicated network. They are constantly sending signals to each other and forming connections with each other. This is how your brain remembers things, does calculations, makes decisions and thinks up ideas. (You can find out more about this on pages 50-51.)

This is a microscope photo of just a few of the huge network of connector neurons inside a human brain.

Amazing neurons

• You have over 100 billion neurons in your body in all.

• Each neuron in the brain can be connected to thousands of others, and can receive over 100,000 signals every second.

• Messages whizz around your nervous system at up to 270mph.

• Neurons that reach from your spinal cord to your toes are the longest cells in the body. They're too narrow to see, but they can be up to 4ft long.

Seeing

The five senses – seeing, hearing, touch, taste and smell – are your brain's tools for detecting the world around you. Seeing is one of the most important senses for humans and most other animals. Your eyeballs collect light patterns and send signals to your brain, and your brain works out what they mean. Sometimes, though, the brain gets it wrong – or even makes up things that aren't really there.

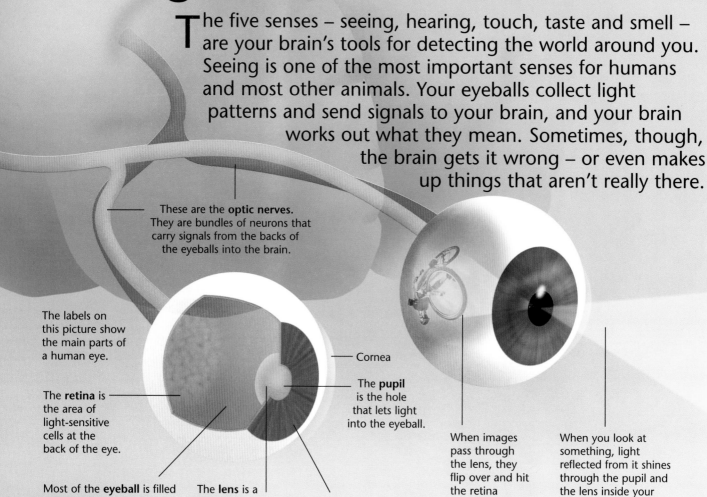

These are the **optic nerves**. They are bundles of neurons that carry signals from the backs of the eyeballs into the brain.

The labels on this picture show the main parts of a human eye.

The **retina** is the area of light-sensitive cells at the back of the eye.

Cornea

The **pupil** is the hole that lets light into the eyeball.

Most of the **eyeball** is filled with a clear, thick jelly called vitreous humor.

The **lens** is a transparent disc just behind the pupil.

The **iris** is the colored part of the eye.

When images pass through the lens, they flip over and hit the retina upside down.

When you look at something, light reflected from it shines through the pupil and the lens inside your eye, and hits the back of your eyeball.

Amazing eyeballs

Your eyeballs are the sense organs that let you see. They collect light patterns and turn them into signals, ready to send to the brain. Each eyeball contains a lens that focuses images onto the back of the eyeball.

INTERNET LINK

For a link to a website where you can do lots of online experiments to do with vision, go to www.usborne.com/quicklinks

Cells for seeing

Inside the back of each eyeball is a patch of light-sensitive cells called the retina. It is made of over 100 million "rod" cells, which detect white light, and about six million "cone" cells, which detect red, blue or green light (so you can see in color). Each cell converts the light it detects into an electrical signal, which is then carried along the optic nerve and into the brain.

Into the brain

Because your eyes are so near your brain, the signals don't need to travel up your spine to get there. Instead, the optic nerve leads right into the brain from the back of each eyeball. Each optic nerve is made up of millions of neurons, all connected to the light-sensitive rod and cone cells. The optic nerves send the signals to the visual cortex – the part of the brain that processes images.

The brain's job

As soon as the brain receives light signals from the optic nerve, it starts to interpret them (work them out). Firstly, it flips images right side up, so they make sense. Then, it decides what you can see. It matches shapes and movements against images in its memory, so you can understand what's going on around you.

When you look at this picture, you actually see the wheels as two ovals. But your brain recognizes them as two round wheels seen from different angles, and tells you that you are seeing a bike.

Bossy brain

Sometimes, the brain takes over and sees only what it wants or expects to see. Try this experiment:

PARIS
IN THE
THE SPRING

Did you see the second "THE"? Most people don't the first time around, because their brain decides it's useless and ignores it.

GOING WRONG: Color blindness

The retina has different types of cone cells for detecting different colors. Most people's eyes can see a wide range of colors.

In color-blind people, there are fewer types of cone cells. This usually makes it hard for them to tell the difference between red and green, especially in dim light. Scientists have found that most color-blind people are male.

This is a color blindness test. If you can see a number in the circle, you're probably not color-blind. If you can't, it may be because you are color-blind and find it hard to tell the difference between green and red.

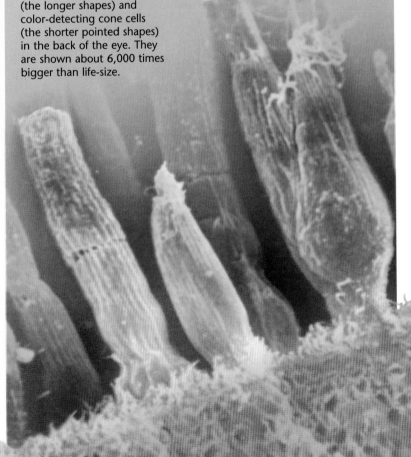

This is a microscope photo of light-detecting rod cells (the longer shapes) and color-detecting cone cells (the shorter pointed shapes) in the back of the eye. They are shown about 6,000 times bigger than life-size.

Hearing

There's a lot more to your ears than meets the eye. The part you can see, attached to your head, is called the pinna, or outer ear. It's just the start of a sequence of parts leading into your head. Together, they turn sounds into signals your brain can understand.

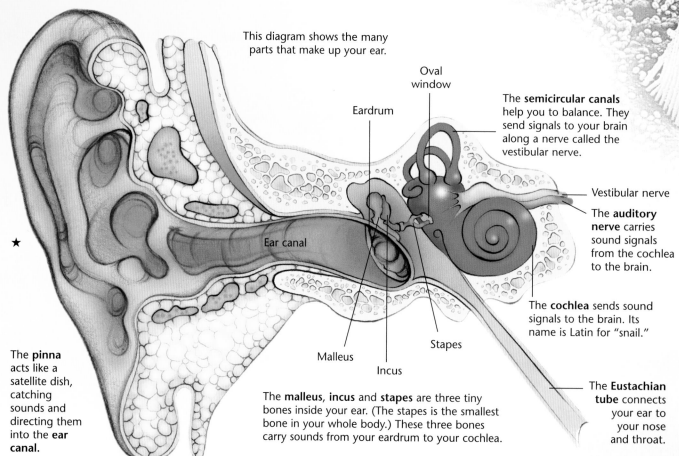

This diagram shows the many parts that make up your ear.

Oval window

Eardrum

The **semicircular canals** help you to balance. They send signals to your brain along a nerve called the vestibular nerve.

Vestibular nerve

The **auditory nerve** carries sound signals from the cochlea to the brain.

Ear canal

The **cochlea** sends sound signals to the brain. Its name is Latin for "snail."

Stapes

Malleus

Incus

The **pinna** acts like a satellite dish, catching sounds and directing them into the **ear canal**.

The **malleus**, **incus** and **stapes** are three tiny bones inside your ear. (The stapes is the smallest bone in your whole body.) These three bones carry sounds from your eardrum to your cochlea.

The **Eustachian tube** connects your ear to your nose and throat.

Sounds into signals

Every sound you can hear is made up of sound waves. Sound waves work by making tiny particles of air vibrate back and forth. The particles bump into each other, making the sound waves spread through the air and into your ears. Here's what happens when your ears hear a sound:

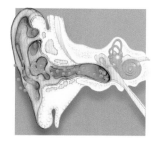

1 Air vibrations enter your ear and travel along your ear canal. They hit your eardrum and make it vibrate too.

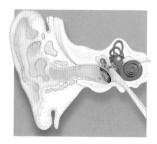

2 The vibrations pass from the eardrum along the malleus, incus and stapes, through the oval window and into the cochlea.

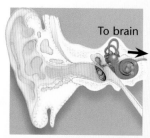

To brain

3 Tiny hairs inside the cochlea detect the vibrations. They turn them into electrical signals and send them to your brain.

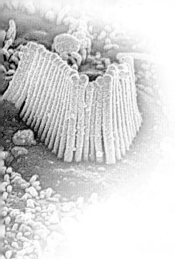

This microscope photo shows clumps of sensitive hairs inside your cochlea, at about 12,000 times life-size.

This patient is having her ear syringed. The wax will be flushed out of her ear into the bowl.

GOING WRONG: Ear wax

Your ears make wax to protect themselves from water and dirt. Sometimes, too much ear wax can collect in your ear and block your ear canal, making you deaf. A doctor or nurse may have to squirt water into your ear with a syringe to force the wax out.

Volume and pitch

Louder sounds make bigger vibrations in the air. Your ear can tell how loud a sound is by the size of the vibrations. High-pitched sounds make fast vibrations, and low-pitched sounds make slow ones. Your cochlea has different types of hairs which are sensitive to different vibration speeds. By checking which hairs have been set off, your brain can work out how high or low a sound is.

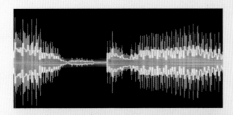

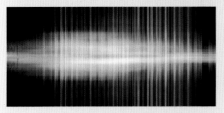

These computer displays show the different kinds of sound wave patterns made by two different voices. We can recognize people's voices because our brains can tell the difference between different sound wave patterns.

Balancing

As well as hearing, your ears help you balance. Next to the cochlea is a set of tubes called the semicircular canals. As you move around or tilt your body, liquid inside these tubes swirls around and makes tiny hairs bend.

Like your hearing hairs, balancing hairs are attached to neurons leading to your brain. They tell the brain what angle you are at so you can keep your balance.

Dogon people from Mali balancing on stilts as part of a traditional ceremony

Tasting and smelling

Taste and smell are important senses. They help you detect danger, by tasting whether the food you're eating has gone bad, or by smelling smoke if your house is on fire. Tasting and smelling are also closely connected to your emotions, and can often bring back memories.

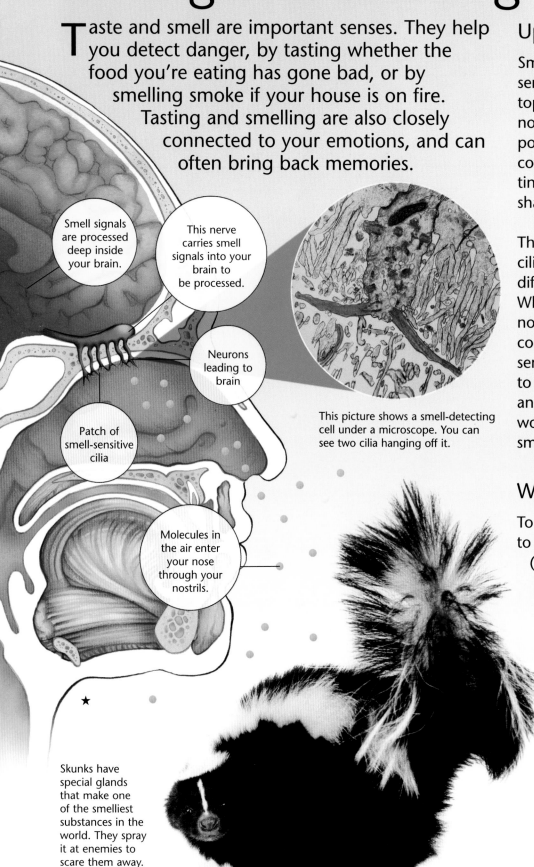

Smell signals are processed deep inside your brain.

This nerve carries smell signals into your brain to be processed.

Neurons leading to brain

Patch of smell-sensitive cilia

Molecules in the air enter your nose through your nostrils.

This picture shows a smell-detecting cell under a microscope. You can see two cilia hanging off it.

Skunks have special glands that make one of the smelliest substances in the world. They spray it at enemies to scare them away.

Up your nose

Smelling is done by a sensitive patch of cells at the top of the inside of your nose. It's only the size of a postage stamp, but it's covered in over 200 million tiny, dangling thread-like shapes, called cilia.

There are about 20 types of cilia. Each one detects different types of smells. When a smell wafts up your nose, it triggers a particular combination of cilia. They send signals along neurons to your brain, and your brain analyzes the information to work out exactly what the smell is.

What is a smell?

To set them off, the cilia have to be touched by molecules (tiny particles) of the substance you're sniffing. A smell is really just a few molecules of something smelly that have floated away from it and found their way up your nose – whether it's stinky cheese, expensive perfume, or a dog mess on the ground. When you sniff at something to get a better smell, you're simply breathing extra bits of it up your nose.

Taste buds

The tongue does its tasting using taste buds. They are found in the papillae – the bumps you can see when you look at your tongue in the mirror. Each taste bud contains nerve endings that are sensitive to different tastes.

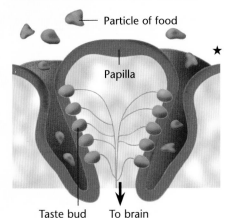

Particle of food

Papilla

Taste bud   To brain

This diagram shows a tiny papilla on your tongue, containing many taste buds.

When you eat, pieces of food enter the small gaps around your papillae and touch the taste buds. As soon as the taste buds detect a taste, they send a signal to your brain.

BODY SCIENCE: **Synesthesia**

Some people get their senses all mixed up. This strange condition is called synesthesia (Greek for "together-senses"). For example, when a synesthetic person tastes an orange drink, she may see flashing lights. When she hears a sound, such as a bell ringing, she may experience a touch or color sensation too.

Tasting team

Most scientists say the tongue can detect four main tastes: sweetness, saltiness, sourness and bitterness. Some think there is also a fifth taste called "umami," or savoriness. But you can taste many more than five flavors, because your nose and tongue work as a team. When you eat, molecules of food waft up your nose, giving you extra clues about what you are tasting. To test this, try eating food while holding your nose. Does it taste the same as usual?

This is a close-up of the surface of a human tongue. The bumps all over it are the papillae.

INTERNET LINK

For a link to a website where you can find out lots more about taste buds and how they work, go to
www.usborne.com/quicklinks

Store of sensations

An average person can detect thousands of different smells and tastes. But how do you know which is which? The answer is that your brain has a huge "library" of different tastes and smells locked away in its memory. Every time a sensation comes in, the brain compares it with its memories to find out whether it's chips or cola, perfume or sweaty socks.

A strong smell from a dead fish can warn you that it has gone bad and is not safe to eat.

Sensation and pain

Touch is usually the last sense people think of, but it's probably the most important. You could manage without sight or hearing, and having a cold or flu can take away your senses of taste and smell. But if you couldn't feel pressure or pain, you'd be in big trouble.

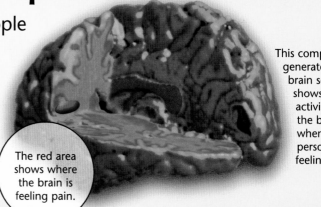

This computer-generated brain scan shows activity in the brain when a person is feeling pain.

The red area shows where the brain is feeling pain.

Skin sensors

You have several different types of touch receptors in your skin. They feel different kinds of sensations, such as heat, cold, pressure and pain. Each receptor is linked to your brain by a long neuron (nerve cell).

When a receptor is triggered, a signal travels along the neuron and up your spinal cord to your brain. Your brain tells you where in the body the signal came from, so you feel as if that's where the sensation is.

The diagram below shows some of the different touch receptors in human skin.

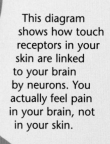

Brain

Neuron

Touch receptor

This diagram shows how touch receptors in your skin are linked to your brain by neurons. You actually feel pain in your brain, not in your skin.

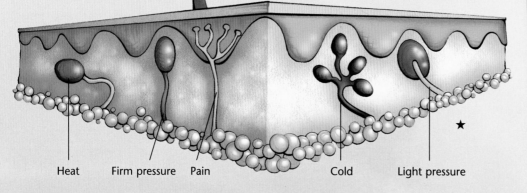

Heat   Firm pressure   Pain   Cold   Light pressure

Sensitive spots

Some body parts are better at feeling than others. Hands, for example, have more touch receptors than knees, and can detect touch sensations more accurately. To test this, ask a friend to close their eyes and guess how many fingers you are pressing against their hand, face or leg.

BODY SCIENCE: Phantom limbs

Some people who've had an arm or leg amputated (cut off) can still sense their missing limb. The limb itself has gone, but the part of the brain that was connected to it still works – so it can "feel" the limb itching or aching.

French athlete Marie-Amélie Le Fur who has had one of her legs amputated competes in the long jump at the Paralympic Games.

Pain override

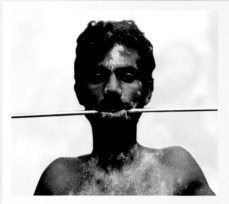

A Hindu man wearing a spike through his face during a religious festival

You can sometimes hurt yourself badly and not feel it. This is because the brain can release chemicals that kill pain for a few minutes. These emergency painkillers can be useful, for example by giving you time to escape from an accident.

Some people even seem to be able to control pain with their minds, allowing them to do amazing tricks like sticking needles through their skin. No one is sure how this works, but it shows you really do feel pain in your brain, not in your body.

No pain, no gain

What's the point of pain? Wouldn't it be better if we didn't have it? In fact, pain is very useful. It's the body's way of warning you something's gone wrong. For example, the pain of a broken leg tells you to keep your leg still and get to hospital. A sharp pain might tell you you've pricked yourself with a pin or have a splinter, and this makes you pull it out.

Where am I?

Special receptors around your joints tell your brain where your body is and what position it's in. This sense of where you are is called proprioception. To test it, shut your eyes and then touch your nose. You can do this because your proprioception receptors tell your brain where all your body parts are.

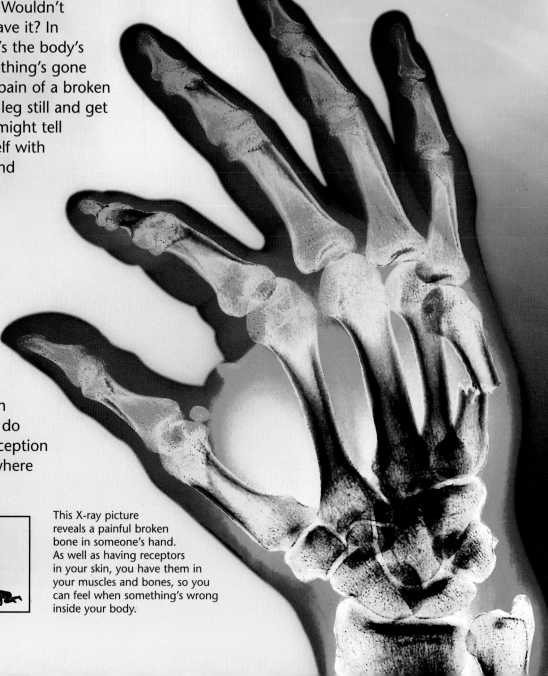

This X-ray picture reveals a painful broken bone in someone's hand. As well as having receptors in your skin, you have them in your muscles and bones, so you can feel when something's wrong inside your body.

INTERNET LINK

For a link to a website where you can find fun experiments to try on your sense of touch, go to
www.usborne.com/quicklinks

Thinking

Your brain has lots of everyday jobs, such as sensing the world around you, checking your temperature and keeping control of your body. However, when people say "Use your brain!", they're usually talking about the brain's other big job – thinking. But what exactly is thinking, and how do you do it?

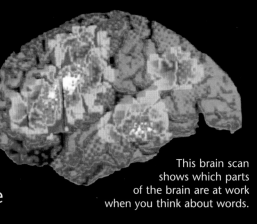

This brain scan shows which parts of the brain are at work when you think about words.

INTERNET LINK

For links to two websites where you can play some games to test your memory, go to
www.usborne.com/quicklinks

Thoughts

When you think, electrical and chemical signals are zooming along complicated pathways inside your brain.

As well as thinking about real life, your brain can put ideas together to make up its own fantasies and stories. This is what's happening when you imagine yourself flying, make up an adventure story or have a daydream.

Consciousness

Instead of just doing its job, like your stomach or liver, the brain is aware of its own thoughts. This awareness is called consciousness. It lets you think things like "Who am I?", "I'm excited" or "I don't want to go swimming." Consciousness is one of the biggest puzzles in science. Experts don't yet know how it happens, or where in the brain it can be found.

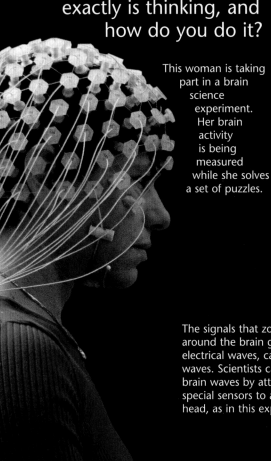

This woman is taking part in a brain science experiment. Her brain activity is being measured while she solves a set of puzzles.

The signals that zoom around the brain give off electrical waves, called brain waves. Scientists can measure brain waves by attaching special sensors to a person's head, as in this experiment.

Learning

When you learn something new, or experience something for the first time, it sets off a new pattern of electrical signals between the neurons in your brain, and they make stronger connections with each other.

When you remember the same thing, the same pattern of signals is fired off in your brain – even though you are not having the real-life experience at the time. This is how you can learn things by heart, or recreate a particular experience in your "mind's eye."

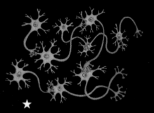

★

1 The brain contains millions of neurons connected together in a huge, tangled network.

★

2 When you learn something, a signal passes through the brain along a chain of neurons.

★

3 The connections between the neurons in the chain get stronger, making a fixed memory.

Memory helps you recognize people. It works so well that you can easily recognize a friend in a huge crowd of people.

Memory

You need to remember all sorts of things all the time – not just things like facts for exams, but also how to walk, talk, tie your shoelaces and recognize your friends. In lots of ways, your memories make you who you are.

You have two main kinds of memory. Short-term memory helps you remember what's happening from one minute to the next. Long-term memory stores important facts and knowledge.

Can computers think?

Sci-fi films often feature computers and robots that are as intelligent as people. But although computers can store lots of facts and do fast calculations, it's very hard to give them consciousness or make them think like humans. However, the science of artificial intelligence (AI) is devoted to making computers better at thinking. One day, they could be as brainy as us.

This robot was developed in Japan to be able to make a variety of different facial expressions. This is an early step on the way to making computerized robots that can respond to and interact with humans.

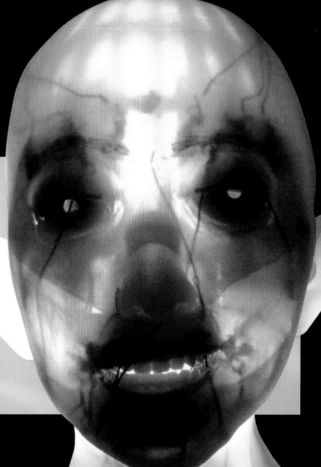

Fool your brain

Your brain might be the most powerful computer in the world, but you can still trick it if you know how. Here are some experiments and illusions to confuse your neurons.

Blind spot

Each eye has a blind spot where the optic nerve sticks through the retina. Try this test to find it. Hold this book up about eight inches from your face. Close your left eye, and focus your right eye on the square. Then slowly move the book closer to you. When the circle is in front of the blind spot of your right eye, it will vanish.

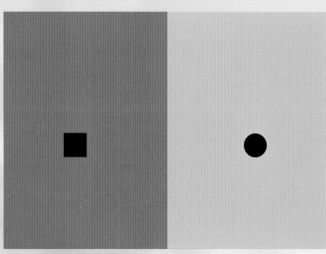

Where the circle was, you see solid yellow, even though there's no yellow there. This is because your brain fills in the space where it can't see anything with the surrounding color. (If you look directly at the circle, you'll see it again, because your blind spot moves as you move your eye.)

INTERNET LINK

For a link to a website where you can find lots more optical illusions to try fooling your brain with, go to www.usborne.com/quicklinks

Optical illusions

Optical illusions are images that trick your sense of sight. Here are two to try:

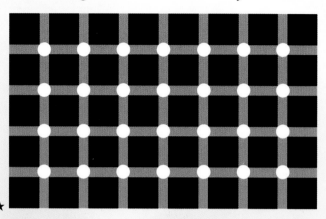

All the round dots in this picture are white. Your brain puts black dots in them because it is confused by the contrast between the white, gray and black areas.

Look at the dot in the middle of this picture, then move your head back and forward. The pattern in the circles makes them appear to move in opposite directions.

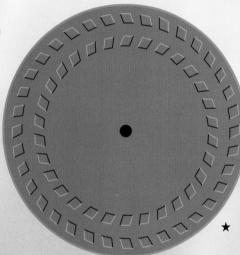

Funny fingers

You can fool your sense of touch too. Cross your first and second fingers, and touch your nose with your crossed fingertips. You only have one nose, but it feels as if you have two. This is because your brain doesn't usually get this kind of signal from these parts of your fingers. It gets confused and thinks you must be feeling two separate things.

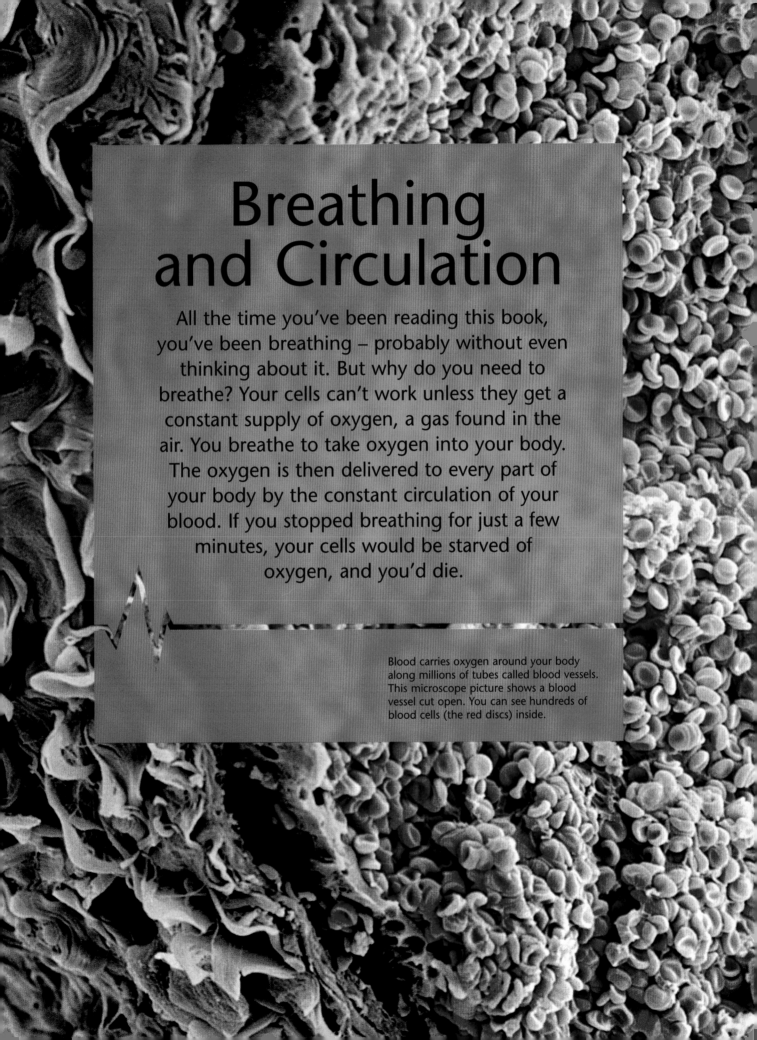

Breathing and Circulation

All the time you've been reading this book, you've been breathing – probably without even thinking about it. But why do you need to breathe? Your cells can't work unless they get a constant supply of oxygen, a gas found in the air. You breathe to take oxygen into your body. The oxygen is then delivered to every part of your body by the constant circulation of your blood. If you stopped breathing for just a few minutes, your cells would be starved of oxygen, and you'd die.

Blood carries oxygen around your body along millions of tubes called blood vessels. This microscope picture shows a blood vessel cut open. You can see hundreds of blood cells (the red discs) inside.

Breathing equipment

Cells need oxygen to give them the energy they need to work. Luckily for them, oxygen is a common gas that makes up 21% of the air surrounding our planet. Your body has a complex set of breathing equipment that takes oxygen from the air and carries it to your cells.

Breathing parts

Oxygen is delivered to your cells by two body systems that work closely together.

The first is the respiratory system. It takes in air and extracts oxygen from it. The respiratory system includes your mouth, nose, throat and trachea (windpipe), and your lungs, two large, spongy bags inside your chest.

The second is the circulatory system. Your blood picks up oxygen molecules from your lungs, and carries them to cells all over your body. The heart pumps blood all around your body, along tubes called blood vessels.

Respiratory system

You breathe air in through your nose or mouth. It then travels down your throat and trachea, and into your lungs.

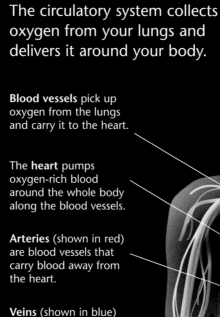

Air enters your body through your mouth or nostrils.

Pharynx (the main part of the throat)

Larynx (part of the throat used for speaking)

The **trachea**, or **windpipe**, is the tube that carries air to your lungs. It has rings of stiff cartilage around it to keep it open at all times.

Lungs take oxygen from the air and pass it into the blood.

Your lungs contain a branching system of millions of tubes, called the **bronchial tree**.

Circulatory system

The circulatory system collects oxygen from your lungs and delivers it around your body.

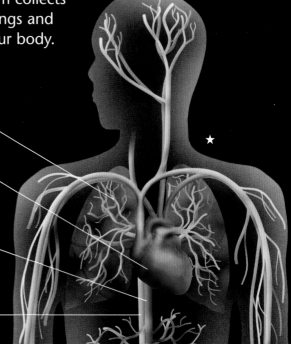

Blood vessels pick up oxygen from the lungs and carry it to the heart.

The **heart** pumps oxygen-rich blood around the whole body along the blood vessels.

Arteries (shown in red) are blood vessels that carry blood away from the heart.

Veins (shown in blue) are blood vessels that carry blood back towards the heart.

INTERNET LINK

For a link to a website where you can see and hear how different speech sounds are made, go to
www.usborne.com/quicklinks

Why oxygen?

You eat food to give you energy, so why do you need oxygen too? Although food does contain energy, it needs to react with oxygen for the energy to be released so that your cells can use it. Here's what happens:

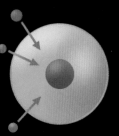

To make energy, your cells take in molecules of hydrogen and carbon from the food you eat, and molecules of oxygen from the air.

This causes a chemical reaction a little like a flame burning. It gives off energy, water, and a gas called carbon dioxide.

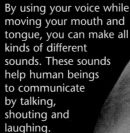

The cells use the energy to do their everyday tasks. The water and carbon dioxide are expelled as waste products.

The carbon dioxide is taken back to the lungs to be breathed out. The spare water escapes from your body in your breath, sweat or urine.

Making a noise

As well as supplying the body with oxygen, breathing has another very useful purpose – it allows us to make noises. Whenever you speak, sing, shout or laugh, air from your lungs is blowing past two stretchy bands in your larynx (throat), called the vocal cords. The moving air makes the vocal cords vibrate, and this makes a sound which we hear as the human voice.

By using your voice while moving your mouth and tongue, you can make all kinds of different sounds. These sounds help human beings to communicate by talking, shouting and laughing.

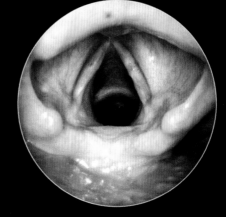

This photo, taken by a tiny camera put down someone's throat, shows the vocal cords and the hole between them where air passes through.

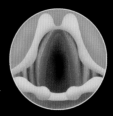

★

To make a high sound, the vocal cords become short and tight.

For a low sound, the vocal cords become longer and looser.

GOING WRONG: Down the wrong way

Your throat acts as a passageway for two very different things – food and air. At the bottom of the throat, there's a flap of muscle called the epiglottis. It covers the windpipe when you swallow, to make sure food doesn't go down into your lungs.

However, if you laugh or move suddenly while you're eating, food can block your windpipe, making you choke. You automatically cough to try to force the blockage out.

Inside your lungs

You couldn't live without your lungs. Their job is to take millions of oxygen molecules out of the air and put them into your blood, ready to be delivered to your cells. At the same time, they take waste gases out of your blood. But how do they do it?

Your trachea is lined with millions of tiny finger shapes called cilia, shown here under a microscope. They catch dust and dirt from the air to stop it from entering your lungs.

In this diagram of a pair of lungs, you can see inside someone's left lung. The right lung is shown with its covering, called the "pleura."

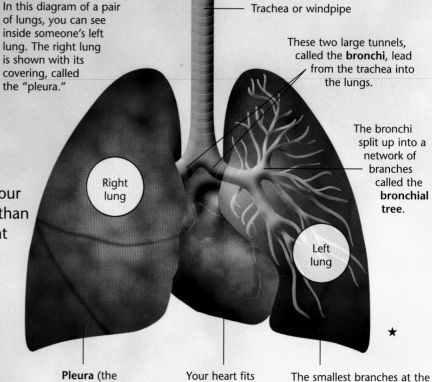

Trachea or windpipe

These two large tunnels, called the **bronchi**, lead from the trachea into the lungs.

The bronchi split up into a network of branches called the **bronchial tree**.

Right lung

Left lung

★

Pleura (the outer covering of the lung)

Your heart fits into a hollow in your left lung.

The smallest branches at the ends of the bronchial tree are called **bronchioles**.

Breathing tree

Your body has two large, spongy, pinkish lungs that fill up most of your chest. The left one is a bit smaller than the right one, because it has a dent in it to make space for your heart.

Inside each lung is a network of thousands of tunnels called the bronchial tree (because it is tree-shaped). The smallest tunnels, at the ends of the tree's branches, are called bronchioles. At the ends of the bronchioles are six million tiny bags called alveoli.

Each bronchiole ends in a cluster of many alveoli.

This is one alveolus.

Each alveolus is surrounded by tiny blood vessels.

Bronchiole (part of the bronchial tree)

Blood vessels

★

In and out

Your lungs seem to breathe by themselves. In fact, when you breathe in, your lungs are being pulled outward by muscles in your chest. To breathe out, the muscles squeeze your chest in again, pushing the air out of your lungs. You can see a diagram showing this on page 27.

56

How lungs work

When you breathe in, each alveolus fills up with air and takes the oxygen from it. The oxygen molecules pass through tiny holes in the alveolus, into the blood vessels all around it. These blood vessels are so small, only one blood cell can go down them at a time. Each blood cell picks up a load of oxygen as it goes past.

In return, your blood cells drop off some waste for the lungs to get rid of. This is mainly carbon dioxide, the waste gas made by your cells as they work. It floats from the blood vessels into the alveoli and up the bronchioles, and comes out in your breath.

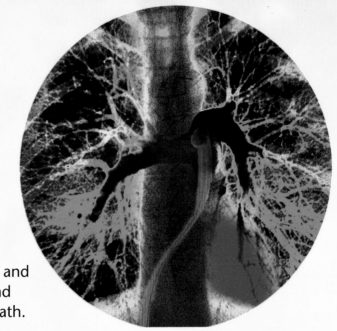

This X-ray shows some of the blood vessels that carry blood in and out of the lungs.

This diagram shows an alveolus and a blood vessel cut in half, so you can see how they work together.

Oxygen

These blood cells are loaded up with oxygen from the alveolus. They are now being carried back to the heart to be pumped around the body.

Alveolus

Blood vessel leading past alveolus

Waste gases

These blood cells are returning from the body. Their oxygen has been used up and they are loaded up with waste gases, which pass into the alveolus to be breathed out.

Blood is pumped into the lungs along blood vessels leading from the heart.

★

Then what?

The oxygen is now in your blood, ready to be sent to your brain, muscles and other body parts. But it doesn't go there immediately. First, the oxygen-rich blood travels along the pulmonary vein and into the heart. You can find out about that on the next page.

INTERNET LINK

For a link to a website where you can hear sounds recorded from healthy and unhealthy human lungs, go to
www.usborne.com/quicklinks

GOING WRONG: Smoke gets in your lungs

Instead of being healthy and pink, a smoker's lungs are dark gray and full of dirt. Chemicals in cigarette smoke damage the cilia in the trachea, so they can't keep dirt out of the lungs. The bronchioles then fill up with tar from the cigarettes, so the lungs don't work very well. Smoking can also cause lung cancer, a dangerous disease which makes lung cells go wrong and start growing out of control.

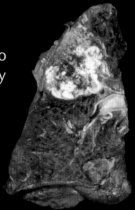

This is a photo of a lung taken from a smoker who died of lung cancer. Instead of being healthy and pink, it is blackened and full of dirt.

The heart

Your heart is an amazingly hard-working muscle. It's only about the size of your fist, but it's strong enough to keep pumping blood around your whole body 24 hours a day, never stopping for a rest. Most of the time, you forget it's even there.

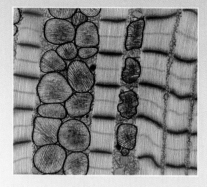

This picture shows a slice of heart muscle through a microscope. The heart is mostly made of muscle.

Where is it?

Your heart is in the front of your chest. It sits between the lungs, and in most people it's slightly to the left side of the body. It's covered with a skin called the pericardium.

Heart halves

The heart has two halves. They do two different jobs, although they work in the same way. Each half has two hollow chambers. One is called the atrium and the other is called the ventricle.

The atrium and ventricle on the left side of your heart fill up with oxygen-rich blood coming from your lungs, and pump it on around your body. The right half of your heart does the opposite job. It fills with used blood, laden down with waste carbon dioxide gas, and pumps it back to your lungs to be cleaned up and given some more oxygen.

This picture shows the inside of the heart and the large blood vessels leading to and from it. By following the numbers, you can see how the heart does its job.

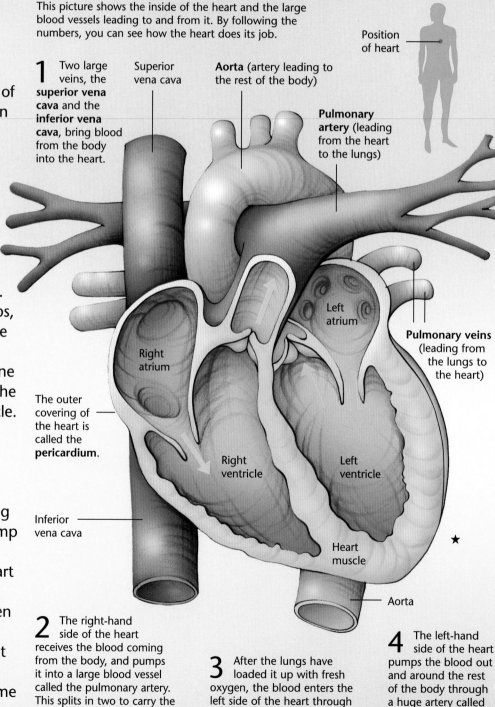

Position of heart

1 Two large veins, the **superior vena cava** and the **inferior vena cava**, bring blood from the body into the heart.

Superior vena cava

Aorta (artery leading to the rest of the body)

Pulmonary artery (leading from the heart to the lungs)

Left atrium

Right atrium

Pulmonary veins (leading from the lungs to the heart)

The outer covering of the heart is called the **pericardium**.

Right ventricle

Left ventricle

Inferior vena cava

Heart muscle

★

Aorta

2 The right-hand side of the heart receives the blood coming from the body, and pumps it into a large blood vessel called the pulmonary artery. This splits in two to carry the blood to your two lungs.

3 After the lungs have loaded it up with fresh oxygen, the blood enters the left side of the heart through the pulmonary veins.

4 The left-hand side of the heart pumps the blood out and around the rest of the body through a huge artery called the aorta.

Powerful pump

But how does the heart actually do its pumping? As the heart is a muscle, it works by contracting (getting smaller) and relaxing. Each time a chamber in the heart relaxes, it opens and fills up with a new supply of blood. Each time it contracts, the blood is squeezed out and toward its destination.

These two diagrams show the heart filling with blood and squeezing it out.

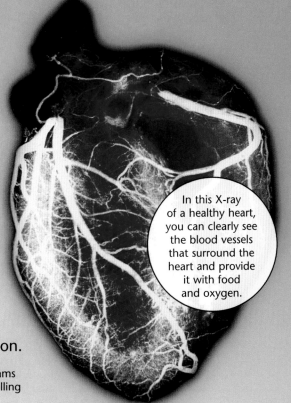

In this X-ray of a healthy heart, you can clearly see the blood vessels that surround the heart and provide it with food and oxygen.

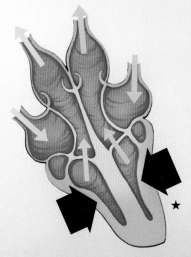

1 The atriums contract, squeezing blood into the larger ventricles.

2 The ventricles contract, squeezing blood into the arteries.

Flapping valves

Your heart has four valves to make sure that when the heart muscle squeezes, the blood goes the right way instead of going back where it came from. Each valve is made of a set of flaps which only open in one direction. If blood tries to move in the other direction, they flap shut.

Valve opens to let blood through.

Valve closes to stop it from coming back.

This flapping makes a "lub-dup" sound – your heartbeat. The "lub" is made by the two big valves in the middle of the heart. The sharper "dup" is made by the two smaller valves at the top of the heart.

GOING WRONG:
Heart attack

The heart has blood vessels all around it. They deliver the food and oxygen the heart needs in order to work. A heart attack happens if one of these blood vessels is blocked by a blood clot (a hard lump of blood). If the blockage is big, your heart runs out of fuel and stops working.

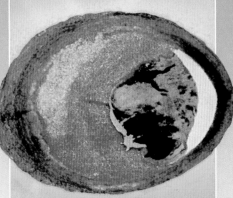

This is a cross section of a heart artery containing a build-up of fat. This makes a heart attack more likely, as a blood clot could easily block the artery.

INTERNET LINK

For links to websites where you can see a heart pumping, hear heart sounds and find amazing heart facts, go to www.usborne.com/quicklinks

Emotions

Lots of people feel as if emotions come from the heart, even though they are really in the brain. This is because feelings like fear and excitement make your heart beat faster and make you breathe more quickly, in case you need extra oxygen to help you act quickly or run away.

Circulation

Circulation means going around and around – and that's what blood does inside your body. You have a network of thousands of miles of blood vessels reaching to every part of your body, so that your blood can carry oxygen and food to every single cell.

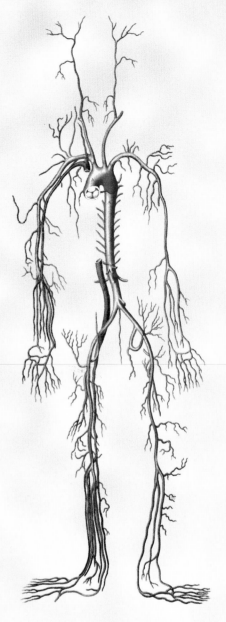

This drawing, dating from 1837, shows some of the body's main arteries and a few of the veins. Near the top you can see the aorta, the largest artery in the body.

Delivery system

As well as taking food and oxygen to your cells, blood carries all kinds of other things around your body. It visits your kidneys to drop off waste chemicals. It carries hormones, which give different parts of your body instructions, such as "grow some hair." And if you take a drug, such as a painkiller, your blood will carry it to the right place. Whatever it's carrying, each blood cell only takes around 20 seconds to make its deliveries and travel back to the heart.

Blood vessels

Blood vessels are the tubes that blood travels along. There are two main types: arteries and veins. Arteries carry blood away from your heart to its destination somewhere in your body. Veins carry blood back to the heart.

In pictures, arteries are usually red and veins are blue. This is because the oxygen-rich blood in arteries is redder. The blood in your veins has had its oxygen used up, and this gives it a darker, purplish color.

From the heart

This picture shows how blood cells travel down smaller and smaller arteries as they move away from the heart. After dropping off oxygen at a cell, the blood cells travel up bigger and bigger veins on their way back to the heart.

Aorta

The **aorta** is the biggest artery. It leads directly out of the heart.

The biggest vein, which leads back into the heart, is called the **vena cava**.

Vena cava

Back to the heart

Blood cells carrying oxygen away from the heart

Large artery

Large arteries lead off the aorta, and branch into smaller arteries.

Large vein

Oxygen-depleted blood cells returning to the heart

Feeling a pulse

Every time your heart beats, or contracts, arteries all over your body swell slightly as blood surges through them. You can feel this surge, or pulse, at several points in your body, such as your wrist.

A friend can feel your pulse by pressing his or her fingers on your wrist, just below your thumb.

INTERNET LINK

For a link to a website where you can watch a movie about the circulation of the blood, go to www.usborne.com/quicklinks

The handover

After leaving your heart, your blood ends up in a network of tiny blood vessels called capillaries, which lie between your cells. The blood travels along the capillaries, releasing oxygen, food and other chemicals, which float out of the capillary walls and into the cells. Waste chemicals from the cells float the other way, out of the cells and back into the blood.

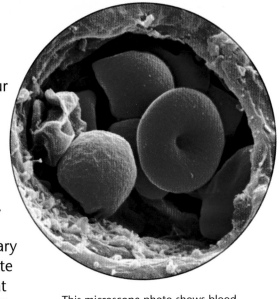

This microscope photo shows blood cells inside a capillary. The capillary is only one or two blood cells wide.

Up the hill

On its way back to the heart, your blood can have a tough job fighting the force of gravity. Even though your heart is still pumping it onward, blood starts to slow down as it makes its way up the veins in your legs and arms. To help it along, veins have valves in them, similar to the valves in your heart. With each heartbeat, the valves open to let blood through, then close to stop it from slipping back down.

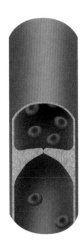

★

Vein valve opens to let blood move uphill on its way back to your heart.

Vein valve closes to stop blood from being pulled back down by gravity.

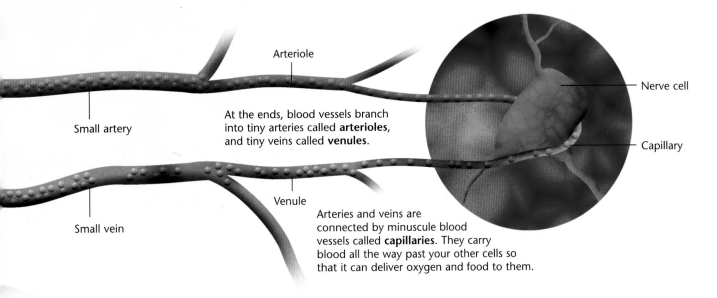

Arteriole

Small artery

At the ends, blood vessels branch into tiny arteries called **arterioles**, and tiny veins called **venules**.

Venule

Small vein

Arteries and veins are connected by minuscule blood vessels called **capillaries**. They carry blood all the way past your other cells so that it can deliver oxygen and food to them.

Nerve cell

Capillary

In the blood

Blood does a vital job as your body's delivery system, carrying food, oxygen and waste to and fro. But what is blood actually made of, and how does it work? These two pages take a closer look at your blood, so you can find out about its interesting ingredients and amazing abilities.

The human blood in this test tube has been separated into its different parts.

What's in blood?

Blood is made up of four main ingredients. The first is a liquid called plasma. It's 90% water, mixed with protein and salt molecules. Plasma carries food chemicals, waste products, and warmth around the body. Floating in the plasma are three types of blood cells. In a drop of blood this big... 🩸 there are roughly:

• 250 million red blood cells, which carry oxygen around the body. They look like flattened balls with a dimple in each side. They are bright red and give blood its color.

• 13 million platelets (also called thrombocytes). These are really just parts of cells. They help your blood clot when you cut yourself.

• 375,000 white blood cells. They're like an army of soldiers, fighting germs that get into the body. They are part of your immune system (see page 80).

A red blood cell's life

The average person has about nine pints of blood rushing around their body, containing about 25 trillion red blood cells. Each individual red blood cell lives for about four months. They start life in your bones, where two million of them are made every second. As new blood cells join the bloodstream, old blood cells go to your liver or spleen to be broken down and turned into waste.

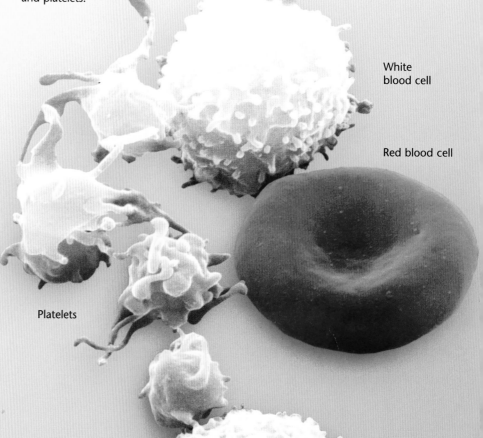

This is a microscope picture of the three types of blood cells: red blood cells, white blood cells and platelets.

White blood cell

Red blood cell

Platelets

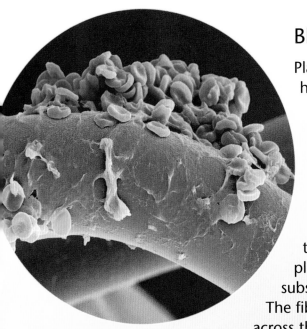

This microscope picture shows blood cells clumping together to form a clot inside the body.

Blood shortage

If you sit in a squashed-up position, your feet might not get enough blood. Your body tells you something's wrong by giving you pins and needles. If you stand up too quickly, you might feel faint or dizzy as your brain goes short of blood for a few seconds.

Your body recovers from these things quite quickly. But if you actually lose blood, from an injury for example, it takes your body a few weeks to replace it. And if you lost more than a third of your blood at once, you probably wouldn't survive.

INTERNET LINK

For a link to a website where you can find games, quizzes and screensavers all to do with blood, go to **www.usborne.com/quicklinks**

Blood clots

Platelets in your blood help it to clot, or stick together, to make scabs. If your body senses a cut or other wound, platelets and red blood cells gather around it. They release a chemical that turns some of your plasma into a stringy substance called fibrin. The fibrin makes a net across the wound, and the blood cells get caught in it, forming a scab.

Clots sometimes form deep inside your body too. They can be dangerous if they break away and lodge in an artery in your heart or brain, which can cause a heart attack or a stroke.

Here's what happens when you cut yourself:

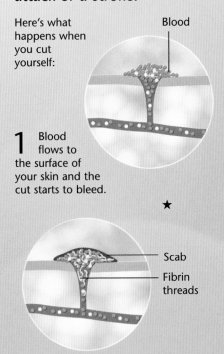

Blood

1 Blood flows to the surface of your skin and the cut starts to bleed.

★

Scab

Fibrin threads

2 The plasma forms stringy fibrin, and the blood cells lump together into a clot. It dries and hardens into a scab.

Hospitals store blood for blood transfusions in plastic bags like this.

BODY SCIENCE:
Blood types

Did you know you might have a different type of blood from your best friend? There are four types of blood, called A, B, AB, and O. They don't look different, but they contain slightly different chemicals.

When someone loses a lot of blood, they can be saved by a blood transfusion – an injection of blood donated by someone else. But it has to be the right type. If a person is injected with the wrong type, their white cells will think the new blood cells are germs, and will try to attack them.

The lymphatic system

Alongside your blood vessels, you have a network of lymph vessels all over your body to drain away liquid. Dotted along them are lumps called lymph nodes, which fight diseases.

The lymphatic system is made up of a network of tubes called lymph vessels, and lumps called lymph nodes.

Leaky tubes

Your blood vessels constantly leak liquid into the spaces between your cells. Cells need some moisture in order to work, but the surplus, called lymph, seeps into the lymph vessels to be recycled. At the top of your chest, the lymph flows back into your blood.

Lymph nodes

Some of your lymph vessels contain bean-shaped lumps called lymph nodes. There are clusters of them in your armpits, neck and major organs.The lymph nodes are full of white blood cells that attack harmful bacteria. So if any germs have found their way into your lymph, they get caught by the lymph nodes before they can reenter your blood.

This microscope picture shows the germ-fighting cells inside a lymph node.

Swollen "glands"

When you're unwell, your lymph nodes work extra-hard at fighting germs to help you get better. This can make them swell up and feel sore. This is what happens when you have "swollen glands" – but the swellings are really lymph nodes, not glands.

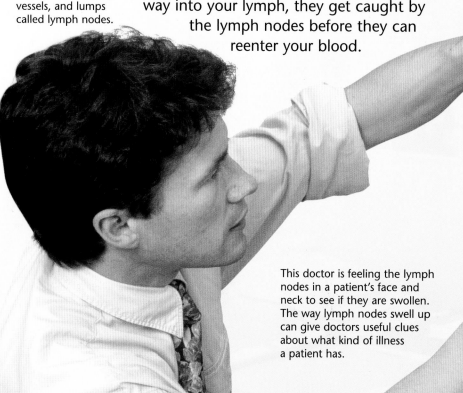

This doctor is feeling the lymph nodes in a patient's face and neck to see if they are swollen. The way lymph nodes swell up can give doctors useful clues about what kind of illness a patient has.

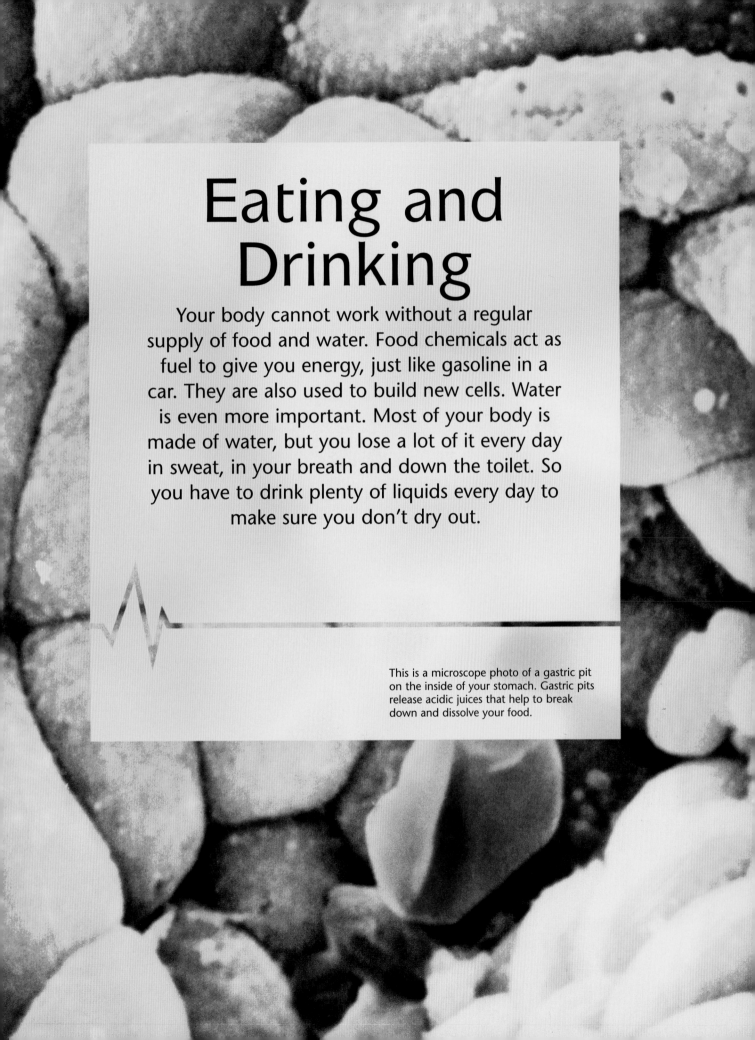

Eating and Drinking

Your body cannot work without a regular supply of food and water. Food chemicals act as fuel to give you energy, just like gasoline in a car. They are also used to build new cells. Water is even more important. Most of your body is made of water, but you lose a lot of it every day in sweat, in your breath and down the toilet. So you have to drink plenty of liquids every day to make sure you don't dry out.

This is a microscope photo of a gastric pit on the inside of your stomach. Gastric pits release acidic juices that help to break down and dissolve your food.

Taking in food

Have you ever wondered why you eat and drink? Apart from tasting good, food is essential to your body. It gives your cells energy for all kinds of jobs, such as moving, breathing and thinking. It also provides all the materials your body is made of, such as proteins, minerals and fat.

Food's journey

Everything you eat and drink goes through a series of organs and tubes inside you, called your digestive system. This important body system is like a long tunnel all the way through your body. It breaks food down into smaller and smaller pieces and then into chemicals, and soaks them up into your blood. Whatever is left over at the end comes out when you go to the toilet.

Food facts

• It takes food up to three days to complete its journey all the way through your digestive system.

• An adult's digestive system is about 30ft long – as long as a large classroom.

• An average person takes in about 4.4lbs of food and drink every day. In your lifetime, you will probably consume over 110,000lbs of food. That's the same as eating ten elephants.

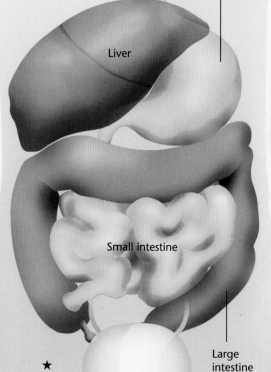

This picture shows the main parts of the digestive system.

The **esophagus** is a tube that carries food from your mouth to your stomach.

Your **liver**, and your **pancreas** and **gall bladder** (not shown in this picture), make juices that help to dissolve and digest your food.

The **stomach** is a stretchy bag that can hold a whole plateful of food. It breaks food down by squeezing it and soaking it in acid.

Liver

From your stomach, food passes into a long, winding tube called the **small intestine**, which extracts useful food chemicals.

Small intestine

Leftover waste travels into the **large intestine**. The large intestine soaks up spare water, collects the leftovers into lumps, and carries them to your bottom.

Large intestine

★

Rectum

The **bladder** stores liquid waste, or urine, until you go to the toilet.

Solid waste leaves your body through a tube called the **rectum**.

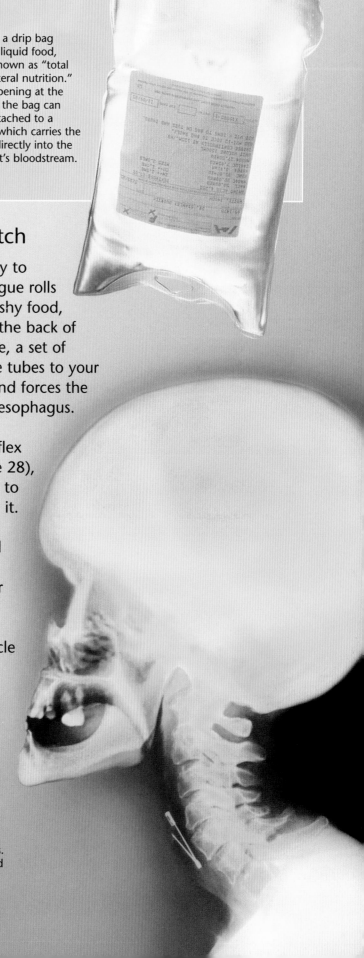

GOING WRONG: Food in a bag

If someone has had a complicated operation on their intestines, they may be unable to eat for several weeks. People who are in a coma can't eat either. Instead, doctors feed a liquid full of food chemicals directly into their blood, through a "central line" – a tube inserted into a large vein in their chest.

This is a drip bag full of liquid food, also known as "total parenteral nutrition." The opening at the top of the bag can be attached to a tube, which carries the food directly into the patient's bloodstream.

In your mouth

Your mouth is a munching machine designed to grind any type of food into a soft pulp.

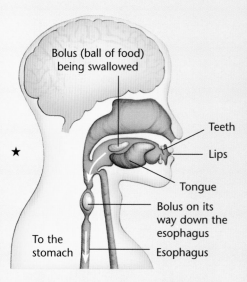

Bolus (ball of food) being swallowed

Teeth

Lips

Tongue

Bolus on its way down the esophagus

To the stomach

Esophagus

As soon as you take a bite of toast, tomato or whatever else you're eating, three mouth mechanisms spring into action:

• Your **teeth** slice and crunch the food up into smaller bits.

• Your **tongue** pushes food around your mouth to make sure your teeth can reach it.

• Your **saliva glands** release saliva (spit), which mixes with the pieces of food to make a wet, gloopy mush.

Down the hatch

When you're ready to swallow, your tongue rolls a small ball of mushy food, called a bolus, to the back of your mouth. There, a set of flaps closes off the tubes to your nose and lungs, and forces the bolus down your esophagus. Once it's started, swallowing is a reflex reaction (see page 28), so you don't have to think about doing it.

Gravity helps food travel down your esophagus to your stomach. Your esophagus also has bands of muscle around it, which squeeze the food along. This means you can eat lying down, or even upside down.

As this X-ray picture shows, the esophagus runs down the neck just in front of the neck bones. This person has swallowed a safety pin, which is lodged in her esophagus.

In your stomach

At the end of your esophagus, lumps of food squeeze through a narrow gap and plop into your stomach – a large, J-shaped, stretchy bag designed to hold an entire dinner. This is where chips, cheese and chocolate start breaking down into the useful chemicals your body really needs.

Inside view

Your stomach is mostly on the left-hand side of your body. In an adult, the empty stomach is about the size of a fist, but a big meal can stretch it to the size of a melon. Food usually spends four or five hours moving through the stomach, from the top end (called the fundus) to the bottom end (the pylorus). As the food moves along, strong muscles squeeze and squish it to grind it down into a mushy soup.

This picture shows a human stomach with the front cut away, so that you can see all its main parts.

The top end of the stomach is called the **fundus**.

The **esophagus** carries food from your mouth into your stomach.

Food is squeezed into your stomach through this hole, called the **lower esophageal sphincter**.

Bolus (ball) of chewed food entering the stomach

Food leaves the stomach through the **pyloric sphincter**.

To the small intestine

This is the **body**, or main part, of the stomach.

Pylorus (bottom end of the stomach)

The stomach usually contains a mixture of mushy food and gastric juice.

The **rugae**, or wrinkles, on the inside of the stomach increase its surface area and allow it to stretch as it gets fuller.

This microscope photo shows one of the gastric pits inside a human stomach, 1,500 times bigger than life-size. Gastric juice comes out of the middle of the pit.

Acid bath

All over the inside of your stomach, there are about three million small holes, called gastric pits. They release a liquid called gastric juice. This juice contains a strong acid and other chemicals which mix with food and help to dissolve it. But why doesn't the acid dissolve your stomach too? The answer is that the stomach is lined with slimy mucus to protect it from the acid. If a piece of stomach does get dissolved, it can repair itself.

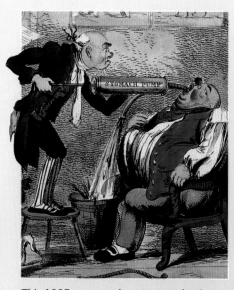

This 1827 cartoon shows a man having the contents of his stomach pumped out. Stomach pumping is still used to remove poison or drugs from the stomach.

GOING WRONG:
Throwing up

If you've ever thrown up, or vomited, you'll know what your stomach contents look like. Vomiting can happen if you eat rotten or poisonous food, if you eat too much, or if you're dizzy, nervous, or unwell. Your stomach squeezes tightly, forcing food up your esophagus and back out of your mouth. When you vomit, the strong stomach acid makes your mouth and nose sting.

Fairground rides can make you dizzy, and may even make you throw up.

Stomach rumbles

You can often hear your stomach making rumbling, squelching and squirting sounds. You can hear these sounds even better if you put your ear right next to someone else's stomach. The noises are made by food and air sloshing around inside the stomach, and being squirted out of the stomach through the pyloric sphincter.

Gases trapped inside your stomach can make similar noises. Sometimes they escape from the stomach, bubble up the esophagus and come out of your mouth as a burp or belch.

INTERNET LINK

For a link to a website where you can find out more about vomiting and how it works, go to
www.usborne.com/quicklinks

Leaving the stomach

By the time your stomach has squashed and squeezed your food for a few hours, and mixed it with acid, it's changed from the mushy balls you swallowed into a thick, creamy mixture called chyme (pronounced "kime.")

The chyme is squirted through the pyloric sphincter, a hole at the bottom end of the stomach, into the next part of your digestive system – your intestines, or guts. You can find out what happens there on the next page.

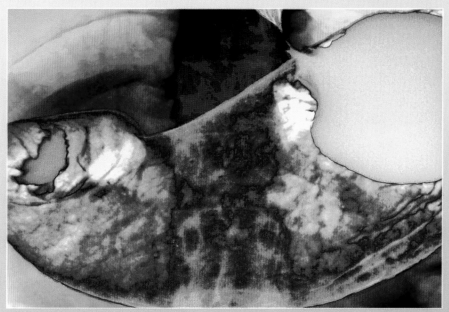

This is an X-ray of a human stomach. The large, pale green blob at the top right is a liquid called barium, which shows up well in X-rays. Patients swallow it before an X-ray, so that doctors can see the digestive system clearly in X-ray pictures.

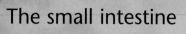

This microscope picture shows the surface of one of the tiny finger-shaped villi inside a small intestine. It's covered with thousands of even tinier finger shapes, called microvilli.

In the intestines

Every single cell in your body needs food in order to keep working. But cells can't make use of food until it has been broken down into tiny molecules. So your intestines – also called guts – prepare food for your cells. They break it down into all the different chemicals it's made of, and pass them into your bloodstream.

The small intestine

From your stomach, liquidized food is squirted into a tube called the small intestine. It's called "small" because it's narrow, but in fact it's very long – about four times the length of your whole body. It's coiled up in a series of loops below your stomach. The small intestine is lined with millions of finger-shaped stalks, called villi. As food is slowly squeezed along, useful chemicals soak into tiny blood vessels inside the villi.

This is a view into a real small intestine. It was taken using an endoscope, a tube which can be inserted into the body to look inside it.

The diagram below shows where the liver, stomach and small intestine are found in your body.

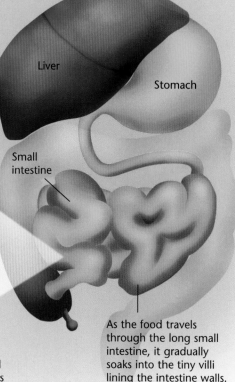

Liver

Stomach

Small intestine

As the food travels through the long small intestine, it gradually soaks into the tiny villi lining the intestine walls.

Food chemicals soak through the surface of each villus and into the blood vessels inside.

Artery carrying blood into villus

Vein carrying food-rich blood away from villus

Through the liver

After entering your blood, the food chemicals go to your liver. This amazing organ has over 500 different jobs. Here are some of the things it does:

• Sorts out the food chemicals your small intestine has collected, and sends them off to different parts of your body.

• Filters out any garbage.

• Makes bile, a liquid your intestines use to digest fat.

• Converts food chemicals into useful body substances.

• Keeps a handy store of spare vitamins and minerals.

What about water?

As well as eating food, you have to drink water or other drinks to stay healthy.

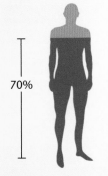

70%

This diagram shows how much of a human body is made of water.

★

Water makes up about 70% of your body, and as it escapes in sweat, breath and urine, you need to replenish it several times a day. Like food chemicals, the water in whatever you eat or drink soaks into your blood through your intestines.

INTERNET LINK

For a link to a website where you can find out which foods make up a good diet, and play a game, go to **www.usborne.com/quicklinks**

Food into fat

What happens if you eat too much food? Your cells only use as much as they need, so what's left over has to be stored. Your liver can store some foods, such as vitamins. But most spare food is turned into fat, which is stored in layers under your skin. You have lots of fat cells there, and they can grow bigger to hold more fat whenever they need to.

Being obese (very fat) can be unhealthy, but you do need some fat under your skin to keep you warm and provide a cushion around your bones.

Obese people, like this man, have a large amount of spare fat stored in their body. It usually builds up most around the abdomen.

BODY SCIENCE: **What's in food?**

Like all substances, food is made up of tiny atoms of different elements. The main elements in food are hydrogen, oxygen, carbon and nitrogen. Different foods can also be divided into these main food groups:

Avocados contain lots of vitamins and fat.

- **Proteins** are found in meat, cheese and beans. They're used to repair the body and build cells.

- **Carbohydrates** are found in sugar and in foods such as bread and pasta. They give your cells energy.

- **Fats** are found in butter, oil and meat, and in foods such as nuts and avocados.

- Many foods also contain small amounts of **vitamins and minerals**. For example, milk contains the mineral calcium, which is used to build bones.

Waste

Not everything you eat ends up being used by your body. All the time, your digestive system is collecting the waste food, water and chemicals you don't need, and storing them for when you go to the toilet. This makes sure the rest of your body stays clean and healthy inside.

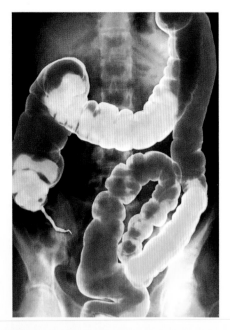

This is an X-ray of a real human large intestine. To make the intestine easy to see, it has been filled with a liquid containing barium, which shows up well in X-rays.

Lumpy leftovers

Once food has passed through your stomach and small intestine, most of the useful food chemicals have been extracted from it. What's left is mostly pieces of food that you can't digest, such as skins, seeds, stalks and other tough parts of fruit and vegetables. They move from the small intestine into the large intestine (also called the bowel or colon).

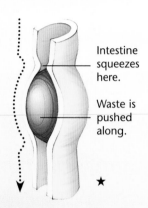

Your large intestine makes a squeezing action to push lumps of waste along. This action is called peristalsis.

Intestine squeezes here.

Waste is pushed along.

★

The tough, leftover waste in your large intestine is called fiber. Although it doesn't provide food, fiber is useful because it helps to sweep your digestive system clean as it moves along. As the fiber and other waste travels past, the large intestine extracts water from it, drying it into solid lumps.

Bowel bacteria

Your large intestine contains millions of bacteria – tiny living organisms that aren't part of your own body at all. They don't usually harm you – in fact, some of them make useful vitamins which help your body. But they do feed on the leftovers in your bowel, so they are growing and breeding there all the time.

When you go to the toilet, lots of these bacteria come out of your rectum along with the leftover food. In fact, up to a third of each lump of waste is made of bacteria.

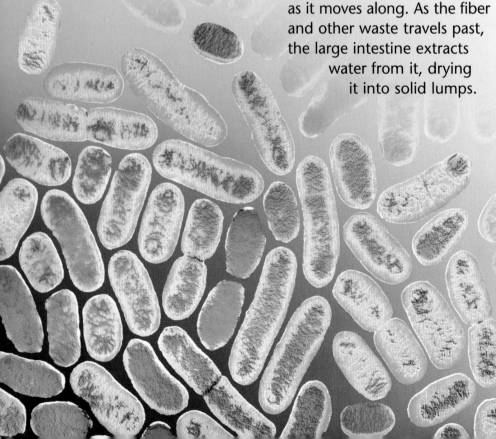

Millions of *E. coli* bacteria like these live in everyone's large intestines. They are usually harmless, but they can make you ill if they get into your food. That's why people wash their hands after going to the toilet.

Waste water

Your body has a separate system to get rid of spare water, along with some waste chemicals from the blood. It's called the urinary system, and its main organs are the kidneys. Most people have two of them. They're in the middle of your back, behind your stomach.

Each kidney contains up to a million tiny filtering units, called nephrons. All the blood in your body goes through your kidneys and through the nephron filters. They take out waste chemicals and spare water, and return the clean blood to your bloodstream.

The urinary system includes two kidneys, a bladder, and all the tubes that lead in and out of them and connect them together.

This blood vessel, the **renal artery**, carries dirty blood into the kidney.

Left kidney cut in half

Right kidney

This blood vessel, the **renal vein**, carries clean blood out of the kidney.

★

The **ureter** is a tube that carries urine from the kidney to the bladder.

The microscopic **nephrons** are found in these sections inside each kidney.

Bladder with a section cut away to show the inside

Urine enters the bladder here.

The bladder stretches and gets bigger as it fills up with urine.

A ring of muscle here keeps the bladder closed most of the time.

The **urethra** carries urine out of the body.

Bladder bag

When the kidneys have done their work, you're left with a smelly, watery liquid called urine. It is collected and stored in your bladder – a tough, stretchy bag at the bottom of your abdomen.

Most of the time, a set of strong muscles holds your bladder and your rectum tightly closed. This means that the waste can be safely stored until you feel like going to the toilet.

GOING WRONG:
Kidney failure

If your kidneys go wrong, poisons can build up in your body, making you ill. People whose kidneys don't work have to have their blood cleaned by a machine called a dialysis machine, or else have a new kidney transplanted. You can survive with just one kidney, so people sometimes donate one of theirs to a relative who needs a kidney transplant.

This doctor is holding a kidney that is waiting to be transplanted into its new owner.

INTERNET LINK

For a link to a website where you can see an animation showing how a kidney transplant works, go to **www.usborne.com/quicklinks**

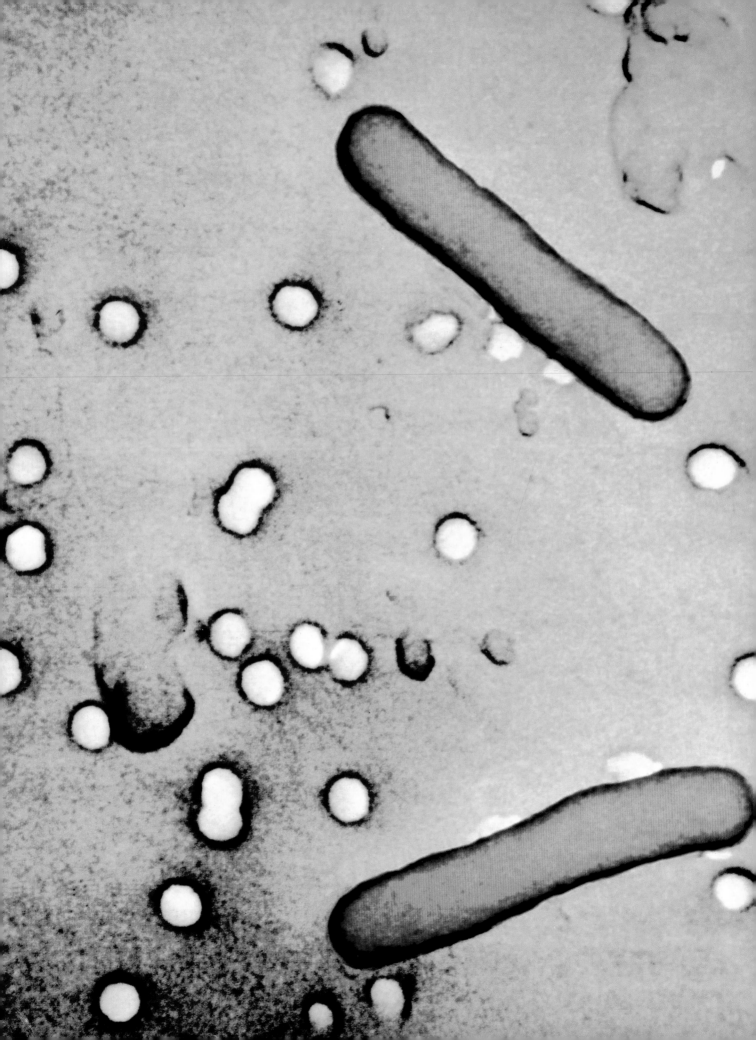

Health and Medicine

The human body is an amazing machine, but it doesn't always work perfectly. Almost everyone gets minor illnesses, such as colds, chicken pox and eczema. Some people are unlucky enough to get a serious disease such as diabetes or cancer. Throughout history, humans have been discovering and developing medicines to cure and prevent diseases, and millions of illnesses, including many serious ones, can now be stopped. Today, more of the world's people are healthy than ever before.

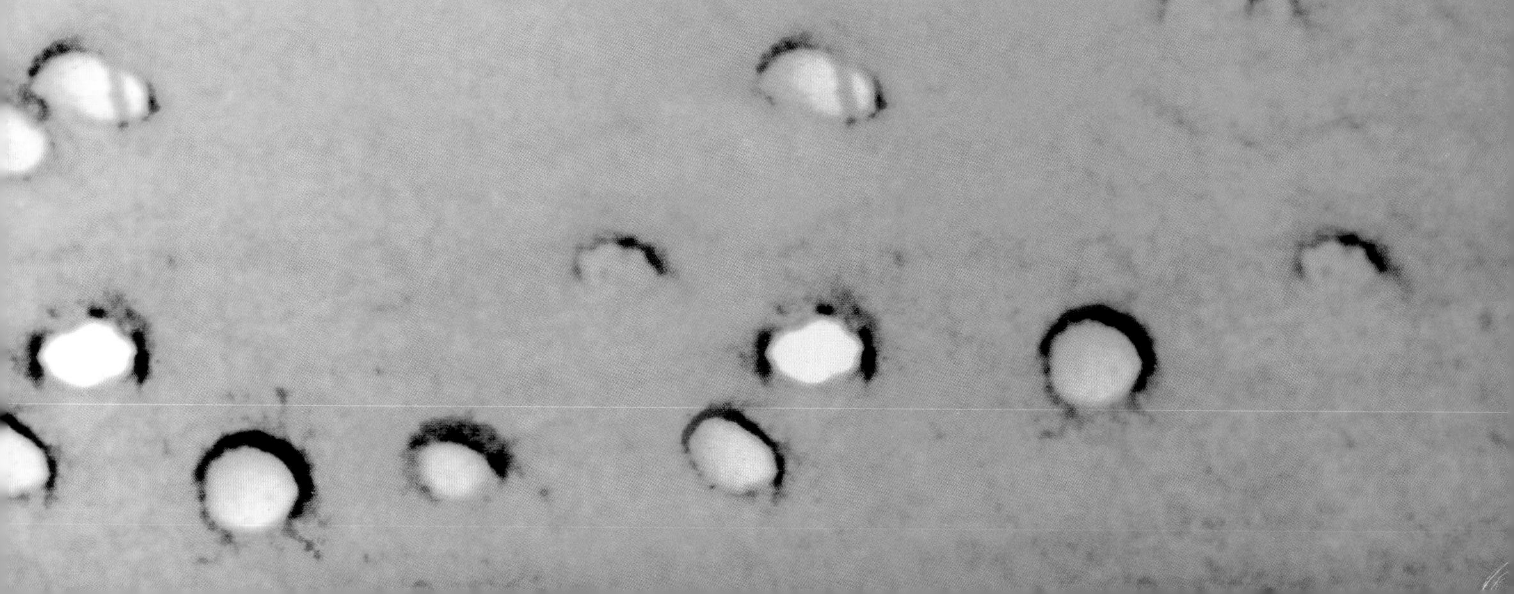

This microscope picture shows *Salmonella* bacteria. They are sometimes found in food, and can make you very sick with food poisoning.

Health and sickness

When you're healthy, it means your body is working properly and you feel good. Unfortunately, though, our bodies can go wrong. The next few pages are all about what happens when you're unwell, and what your body – and your doctor – can do about it.

Staying healthy

Your body can't just stay healthy by itself. It needs good food, clean water, exercise and many other things. Here are the main ingredients for a healthy life:

This X-ray picture shows an area of lung cancer (the orange blob) in a human lung.

• You need **clean water** for washing and drinking, and **a good diet** that includes protein, carbohydrates and fruit and vegetables.

• **Exercise** keeps your heart, blood vessels and muscles healthy.

• **Sleep** helps your body to refresh and repair itself. You spend about a third of your life asleep.

• **Clean, safe surroundings.** People who live in polluted places or work with dangerous chemicals have a much greater chance of getting sick.

• **Sunshine.** Too much sun can damage your skin, but your body needs daylight.

Going wrong

There are lots of things that can go wrong with your body. Here are some of them:

• **Genetic diseases.** Mistakes in your genes cause diseases such as cystic fibrosis.

• **Cancer** happens when some of the cells in your body multiply too fast. It can sometimes be caused by faulty genes.

• **Poor nutrition.** Eating too much, too little, or unhealthy food can make you ill.

• **Organ failure.** Sometimes body organs, such as the heart or kidneys, stop working properly.

• **Injuries.** Your body can be damaged by injuries, such as broken bones, cuts or burns.

• **Allergies** happen when your body reacts badly to something like pollen or cat hair.

• **Mental illnesses.** These affect your moods and the way you behave.

Swimming is a good form of exercise that uses most of the muscles in your body.

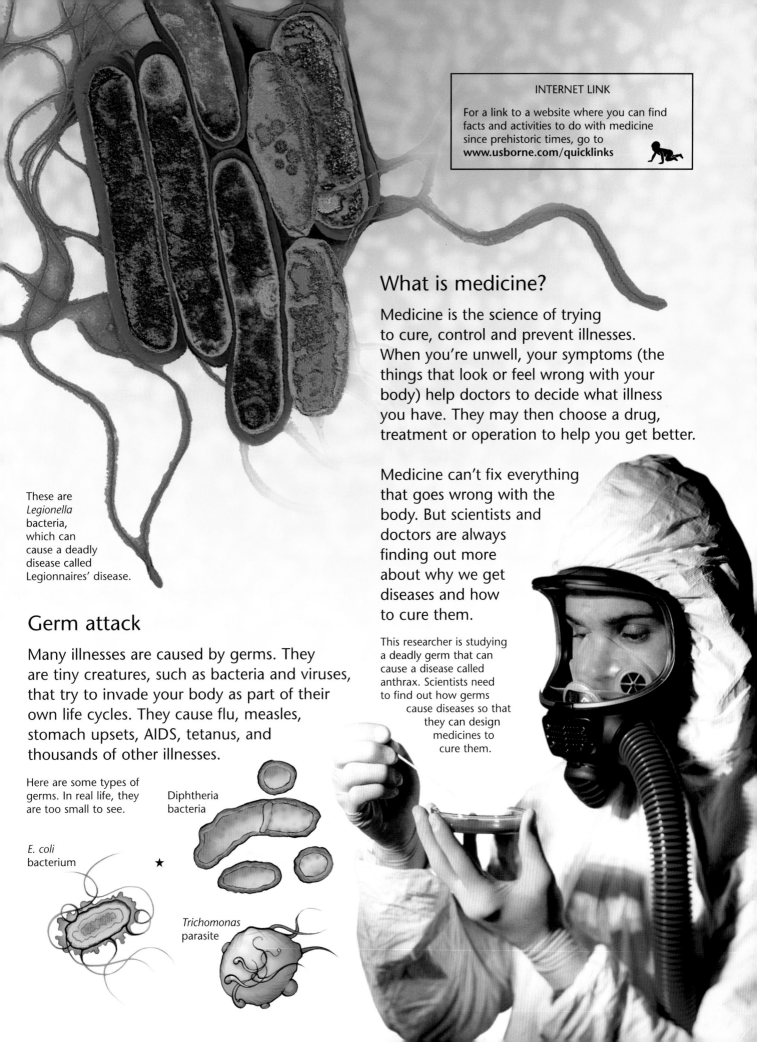

INTERNET LINK

For a link to a website where you can find facts and activities to do with medicine since prehistoric times, go to **www.usborne.com/quicklinks**

These are *Legionella* bacteria, which can cause a deadly disease called Legionnaires' disease.

What is medicine?

Medicine is the science of trying to cure, control and prevent illnesses. When you're unwell, your symptoms (the things that look or feel wrong with your body) help doctors to decide what illness you have. They may then choose a drug, treatment or operation to help you get better.

Medicine can't fix everything that goes wrong with the body. But scientists and doctors are always finding out more about why we get diseases and how to cure them.

This researcher is studying a deadly germ that can cause a disease called anthrax. Scientists need to find out how germs cause diseases so that they can design medicines to cure them.

Germ attack

Many illnesses are caused by germs. They are tiny creatures, such as bacteria and viruses, that try to invade your body as part of their own life cycles. They cause flu, measles, stomach upsets, AIDS, tetanus, and thousands of other illnesses.

Here are some types of germs. In real life, they are too small to see.

Diphtheria bacteria

E. coli bacterium

★

Trichomonas parasite

Diseases

In order to cure diseases, doctors and scientists have to understand how they work. But diseases can be so clever and complicated that some of them still manage to outwit us. These two pages look at some of the most common diseases, and what causes them.

These pictures show how viruses work:

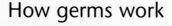

Virus

★

1 A virus attaches itself to the outside of a cell and inserts its genes into the cell.

Genes

2 The genes hijack the cell and instruct it to make lots of copies of the first virus.

3 The new viruses burst out of the cell and infect other cells.

Cell

How germs work

Many diseases are caused by germs that find their way inside your body. Like all living things, germs want to survive. They try to get into your body because it can give them what they need.

• **Bacteria** need food, warmth and moisture, so the body is perfect for them. Millions of bacteria live inside you all the time. Many are harmless, but some can cause illnesses.

• **Viruses** are smaller than bacteria. They invade cells and force them to make more viruses of the same type. Then the new viruses escape to invade other cells. Viruses cause many diseases including colds and chicken pox.

• Other germs include **worms** that like to live inside your body, tiny animals called **protozoa**, and **fungi**, which can give you skin diseases such as athlete's foot.

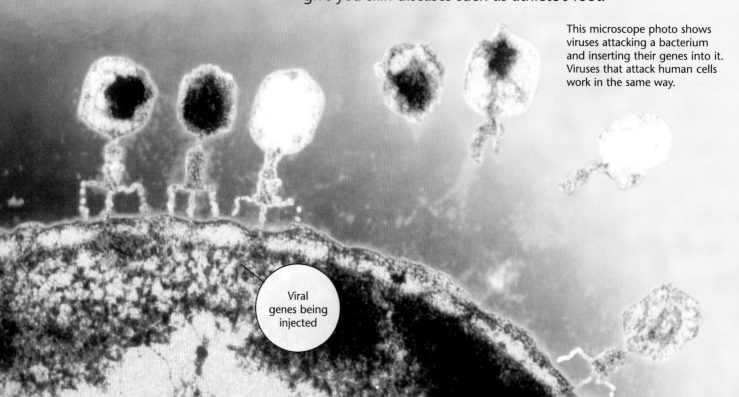

This microscope photo shows viruses attacking a bacterium and inserting their genes into it. Viruses that attack human cells work in the same way.

Viral genes being injected

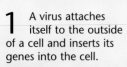

What is cancer?

Cancer is a name for a group of over 100 diseases that affect different parts of the body. It happens when a group of cells starts to grow and reproduce too fast, making a lump called a tumor. Some tumors are "benign," or harmless. But cancer tumors are "malignant," which means they are dangerous. They can spread around the body and invade different organs, stopping them from working.

Cancers are caused by genes inside cells going wrong. This can happen because the cells are irritated or damaged by something like cigarette smoke or asbestos. It's also possible for people to inherit cancer-causing genes from their parents.

This is a microscope picture of a cancer cell. Cancer can sometimes be cured by cutting the cancerous cells out of the body.

Body breakdown

Many illnesses are caused by body parts breaking down. As people get older, their organs begin to weaken and wear out.

This diagram shows how one type of heart disease happens.

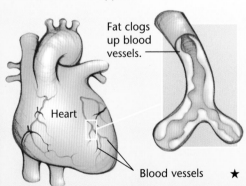

Fat clogs up blood vessels.

Heart

Blood vessels ★

Heart disease is a common type of body breakdown. Fatty lumps clog the blood vessels around the heart, so it's hard for blood to get through. If the blood flow is totally blocked, it can cause a heart attack.

INTERNET LINK

For a link to a website where you can play lots of games to do with different germs, go to www.usborne.com/quicklinks

Genetic diseases

Genes are instructions that tell your cells how to grow and make body substances (see page 14). If you have a genetic disease, it means your genes have mistakes in them and can't make all the chemicals your body needs. For example, people with hemophilia can't make a chemical that helps blood to clot and form scabs. If they cut themselves, they can lose a lot of blood.

BODY SCIENCE:
Spreading diseases

To survive and reproduce, germs have to travel from person to person. They have clever ways of doing this. For example, a cold virus makes you sneeze. This sends a fine spray of mucus (snot), containing copies of the virus, into the air. Other people breathe it in and catch the virus themselves.

This photo shows the pattern of snot droplets sprayed into the air by a sneeze.

The immune system

You're always surrounded by germs, so why aren't you always ill? The answer is your amazing immune system. It's constantly on guard to keep germs, bugs and poisons out of your body. If they do get in, your immune system goes into deadly battle against them.

INTERNET LINK

For a link to a website where you can find out more about what causes allergies, go to **www.usborne.com/quicklinks**

Body barriers

The immune system's first line of defense is your skin. As well as acting as a barrier to germs, skin releases a bacteria-killing acid to zap germs that land on you. However, they can still get in through holes in your body, such as your mouth, nostrils, ears and eyes. To stop them, there are germ-killing chemicals in your saliva (spit), tears, ear wax and even in the mucus (snot) up your nose.

Tears wash germs and dust out of your eyes. They also contain chemicals that kill germs.

White cell battles

Sometimes germs get into your body through cuts and grazes. When this happens, special cells called white blood cells rush to the affected area and destroy as many germs as they can.

The blue blob in this picture is a type of white blood cell. It kills germs by swallowing them up.

These pictures show how a white blood cell kills a germ:

1 A white blood cell closes in on a germ and reaches around it.

White blood cell

Germ ———

2 The white blood cell wraps itself around the germ and sucks it in.

3 The white blood cell surrounds the germ completely, and breaks it down into harmless bits.

★

However, white cells don't always win. If a cut is badly infected with germs, you'll see sticky yellow pus seeping out of it. This is made of the bodies of white blood cells that died in the battle.

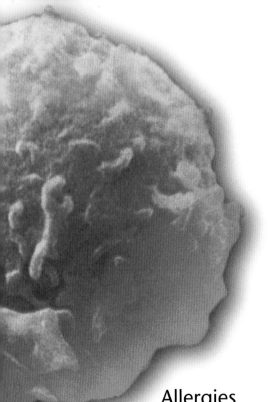

Amazing antibodies

Some white blood cells make chemicals called antibodies, which can protect against bacteria, viruses and poisons. There are millions of different antibodies. Each one is designed to fight a particular type of germ.

Antibodies disable germs by sticking onto them and making them useless.

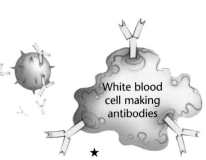

Antibodies

White blood cell making antibodies

Disabled virus

Allergies

An allergy is your immune system making a mistake. It reacts to something harmless, such as pollen, as if it were a germ. Your body then makes lots of a chemical called histamine, which is meant to help your blood vessels release germ-fighting white cells. All the extra histamine can make you sneeze or feel itchy.

If you don't have the antibody for a particular germ, your body may take a while to learn how to make it. This is why you can catch a cold, have it for a week and then get better.

Feeling feverish?

Some types of mosquitoes spread a disease called malaria when they bite. It can give you a very bad fever.

BODY SCIENCE: Vaccination

Most vaccinations work by putting a weakened germ into your body. The germ doesn't make you ill, but your body still learns how to make the antibodies for it. Then, if you catch the real germ, you can fight it off. Vaccinations can protect against diseases such as polio and measles.

This old illustration of a vaccination dates from 1827. Vaccination was first discovered in China in the 10th century.

Sometimes, if you have an illness such as the flu, white blood cells release a chemical called Interleukin-1. It gives you a fever (a high temperature) and makes you feel tired. Your body does this because the extra heat helps to kill germs, while the tiredness makes sure you rest until you're better.

Drugs and treatments

Your immune system does its best to fight diseases, but sometimes it needs help from medical treatments and drugs. They can make you feel better, cure illnesses and even save your life.

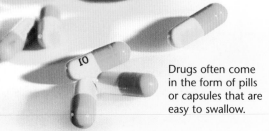

Drugs often come in the form of pills or capsules that are easy to swallow.

What is a drug?

A drug is a chemical that changes the way your body works. There are thousands of drugs with many different effects. For example, aspirin numbs pain, caffeine keeps you awake, and beta blockers slow down your heart.

Medical drugs

Medicines are drugs that are used to treat illnesses. Scientists are always studying different drugs to see if they can be used as medicines.

Antibiotics, for example, which kill bacteria, are very important medicines. Doctors first started using them widely in the 1940s, and since then they have saved millions of people from deadly infections such as whooping cough and TB (short for tuberculosis).

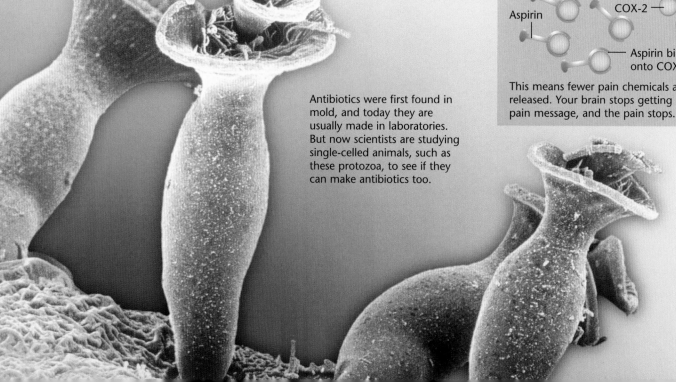

Antibiotics were first found in mold, and today they are usually made in laboratories. But now scientists are studying single-celled animals, such as these protozoa, to see if they can make antibiotics too.

How aspirin works

Unlike an antibiotic, the drug aspirin works by blocking pain messages to your brain. These pictures show how.

When you hurt yourself, your nerves send a "pain" message to your brain.

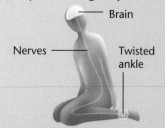

Brain

Nerves

Twisted ankle

A protein called COX-2 helps this to happen. It makes chemicals that tell your nerves to send the "pain" signal.

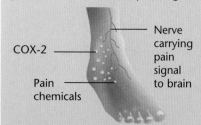

COX-2

Nerve carrying pain signal to brain

Pain chemicals

When you take aspirin, your blood carries aspirin molecules all around your body. They bind onto COX-2 proteins and stop them from working.

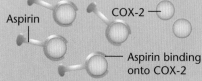

Aspirin

COX-2

Aspirin binding onto COX-2

This means fewer pain chemicals are released. Your brain stops getting the pain message, and the pain stops.

Are drugs dangerous?

Drugs can be harmful if they are used wrongly, and many are addictive. This means your body starts to depend on them and can't manage without them. Some dangerous drugs, such as cocaine, are illegal, but others are part of everyday life.

This old drawing shows tobacco and a man smoking it. Tobacco contains a very addictive drug called nicotine. This is why people who smoke cigarettes can get addicted and find it hard to stop.

BODY SCIENCE: **The placebo effect**

Placebos are fake medicines that contain no drugs at all. New drugs are often tested by seeing if they work better than a placebo. However, scientists have found that even a placebo can make patients feel better. This is called the placebo effect. It suggests that your brain can actually control some illnesses by itself.

More treatments

Besides drugs, doctors use many other treatments and cures. Here are some of them:

• **Radiotherapy** is used for some types of cancer. It uses radiation to kill cancer cells.

• **Topical medicine**, such as eczema cream, is rubbed directly onto the skin.

• A special **diet**, such as a low-fat or sugar-free diet, can help with illnesses such as heart disease or diabetes.

• **Physiotherapy** involves doing specially designed exercises in order to help repair weak or damaged muscles and bones.

• If something's wrong inside your body, you might need an **operation**. You can find out more about this on the next page.

This woman is wearing a Gamma Knife Radiosurgery helmet, used to treat brain cancer. It works by focusing many beams of radiation at a brain tumor to kill it.

Each of the 101 holes in the helmet can aim a separate radiation beam at the part of the brain where the cancer is.

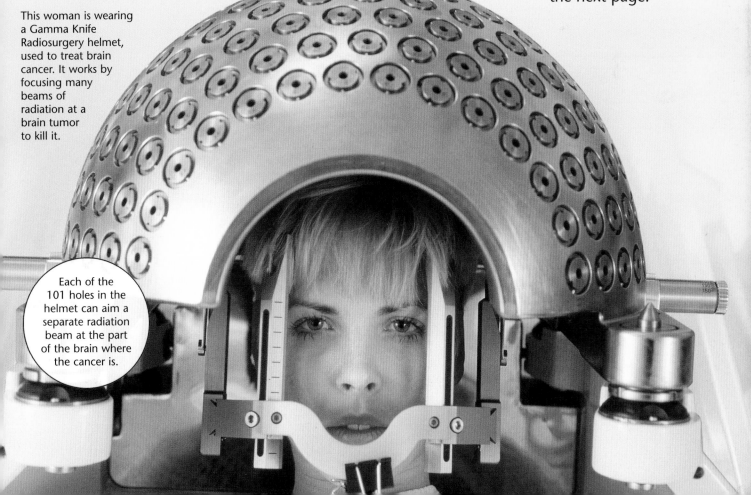

Operations

Sometimes the best way to cure an illness is to open up your body and fix your insides. This is called surgery, or an operation. Operations take place in the hospital, in a room called an operating room. Before the operation, a specially trained doctor called an anesthetist gives the patient a drug called an anesthetic, so he or she won't feel any pain. Then the operating team can start work.

Why operate?

Here are some of the reasons people have operations:

• **Tumor removal.** Tumors are lumps that can grow inside the body. People sometimes have operations to have them cut out.

• **Goodbye appendix.** If you get appendicitis, a body part called the appendix swells up and has to be removed.

• **New body parts.** An organ transplant replaces a bad organ, such as a diseased kidney, with a working one.

• **Heart bypass.** This heart operation replaces a clogged blood vessel with a new one.

• **What's wrong?** Doctors sometimes do operations just to look inside the body to find out if something is wrong.

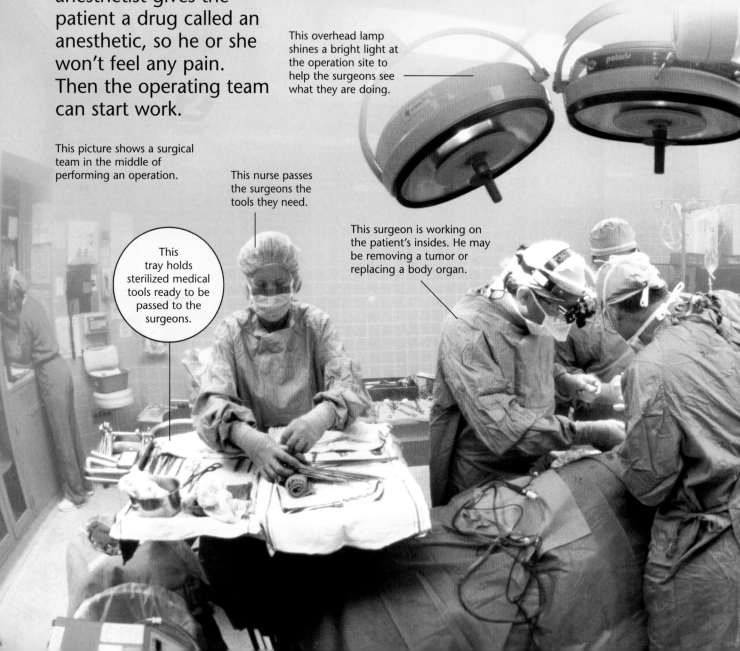

This overhead lamp shines a bright light at the operation site to help the surgeons see what they are doing.

This picture shows a surgical team in the middle of performing an operation.

This nurse passes the surgeons the tools they need.

This tray holds sterilized medical tools ready to be passed to the surgeons.

This surgeon is working on the patient's insides. He may be removing a tumor or replacing a body organ.

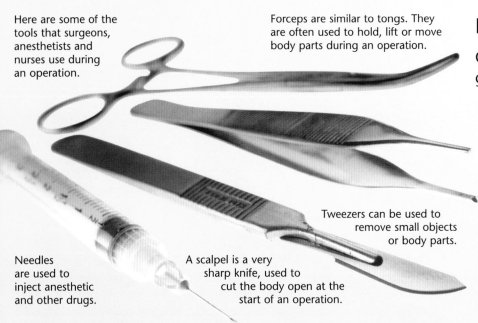

Here are some of the tools that surgeons, anesthetists and nurses use during an operation.

Forceps are similar to tongs. They are often used to hold, lift or move body parts during an operation.

Tweezers can be used to remove small objects or body parts.

Needles are used to inject anesthetic and other drugs.

A scalpel is a very sharp knife, used to cut the body open at the start of an operation.

Bacteria ban

Operations are risky, because germs can get into the body and make the patient even more ill than they were before. So operating rooms and tools must be kept spotlessly clean. The operating team must wash their hands carefully and wear very clean clothes, gloves, hats and face masks.

INTERNET LINK

For a link to a website where you can take a virtual tour of one of the world's oldest operating rooms, go to www.usborne.com/quicklinks

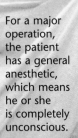

The anesthetist stays near the patient's head and makes sure he or she can't feel anything.

Surgical assistants help the anesthetist to monitor the patient's heart rate and breathing.

For a major operation, the patient has a general anesthetic, which means he or she is completely unconscious.

The patient is covered in a cloth to keep germs away from the operating site.

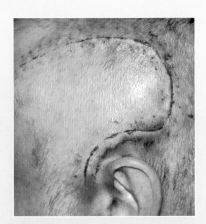

Stitched up

After an operation, the hole is sewn up with special stitches called sutures. People who have had an operation usually have a faded scar where their body was cut open.

This picture shows a fresh post-operative scar on a man's head. It was left by an operation to remove a brain tumor.

Surgery long ago

Until the 1800s, doctors amputated limbs with no anesthetic. The fastest surgeons were the most popular, as the pain was over sooner. Thousands of years ago, people used an operation called trepanning. It involved cutting holes in the skull, perhaps to let out evil spirits that people believed lived in the head.

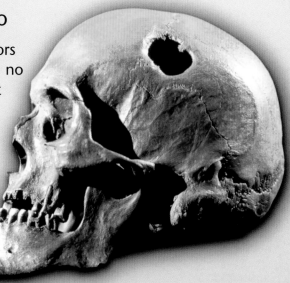

This skull, thought to be about 2,300 years old, was found in Denmark. It belonged to someone who had a trepanning operation while they were alive.

Complementary medicine

The treatments described earlier in this book are all part of "conventional medicine" – the kind you usually get from your doctor. However, many people also get good results from "complementary" medicines. These range from plant remedies to massage, acupuncture and hypnosis.

Acupuncture

Acupuncture is a traditional Chinese medicine. It's based on the idea that a force called chi flows along invisible lines in your body. Acupuncturists insert fine needles into points along these lines to stimulate the body, helping to heal ailments such as back pain.

Some therapists stimulate acupuncture points by burning a herb called moxa on them.

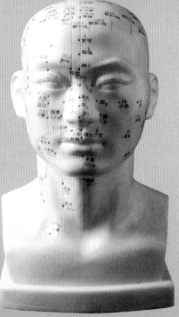

This acupuncture model shows some of the acupuncture points on the head and face.

Does it work?

Complementary medicine is rarely scientifically tested, but it does seem to make many patients feel better. Some treatments, such as acupuncture, are so effective that conventional doctors now prescribe them. However, some experts think complementary medicine works mainly because of the placebo effect (see page 83).

Homeopathy

Homeopathy is a kind of complementary medicine that was invented about 200 years ago. Instead of changing the way your body works, a homeopathic remedy contains a chemical that gives you the illness you have already. But it is diluted so much that only a trace of the chemical remains. It is said to work by stimulating your body to react against the chemical and cure your illness by itself.

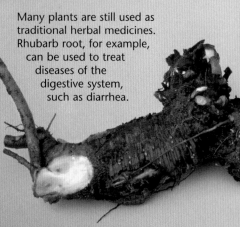

Many plants are still used as traditional herbal medicines. Rhubarb root, for example, can be used to treat diseases of the digestive system, such as diarrhea.

INTERNET LINK

For a link to a website where you can find out more about complementary medicine, go to
www.usborne.com/quicklinks

Body Changes

As you go through life, your body changes. You start by growing from a single cell into a newborn baby, and then continue to grow for the next 20 years, changing from a child into an adult. If you're female, your body may change a lot as it expands to let a new baby grow inside it. From the age of 30, your body starts to shrink. As you grow old, your bones become weaker, your skin wrinkles and your senses become less acute.

This microscope picture shows part of the pituitary gland. It's a gland in your brain that releases chemicals called growth hormones, which make your body get bigger as you grow up.

Conception and birth

Your body is changing all the time, from the moment life begins. Between conception – the moment life starts – and birth, you grow over five million times bigger as you change from a single cell to a newborn human being.

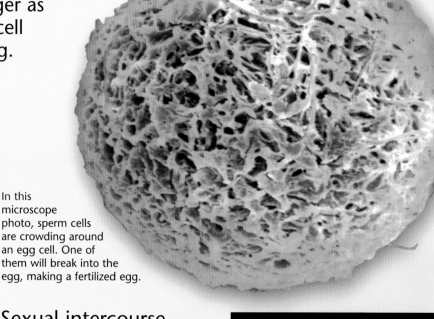

Conception

Conception happens when two cells, one from a man and one from a woman, join together to make a new cell that can grow into a baby.

The cells that can do this are called reproductive cells. Male reproductive cells are called sperm cells, and female ones are called egg cells.

Sperm and eggs have only 23 chromosomes each, not 46 like normal body cells (see page 14). When they join together they make a whole cell called a fertilized egg, which can grow into a baby.

In this microscope photo, sperm cells are crowding around an egg cell. One of them will break into the egg, making a fertilized egg.

Sexual intercourse

So how do a sperm and an egg join up? The main way is called sexual intercourse, or sex. Men and women have different sex organs. They fit together so that sperm cells can get into a woman's body and join up with an egg cell.

The man's main sex organ is the penis. During sex, it fits inside a woman's vagina, a tube between her legs. Sperm cells travel out of the penis and up the vagina. If a sperm cell meets an egg cell inside the woman's body, they join up and make a fertilized egg. It moves into the womb, an organ in the woman's body, to grow into a baby.

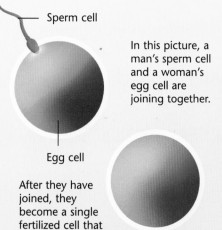

Sperm cell

In this picture, a man's sperm cell and a woman's egg cell are joining together.

Egg cell

After they have joined, they become a single fertilized cell that can turn into a baby. ★

BODY SCIENCE:
Test tube babies

Test tube babies are made by joining sperm and egg cells together in a glass container. The fertilized egg is then placed in a woman's womb. When people's sperm or eggs don't work properly, doctors can do this to help them have a baby.

An egg cell being held on a pipette, ready to be joined with a sperm cell

Being pregnant

When a woman has a baby growing inside her, she is pregnant. The baby lives in the mother's womb for about nine months, and takes food and oxygen from her body. So the mother has to eat and breathe for two living things (or more if she's having twins or triplets).

As the baby gets bigger, the womb swells up to more than 20 times its normal size, and the woman's other organs can get very squashed. Meanwhile, her body makes hormones (see page 92) to help the baby grow. They can make the mother feel sick and dizzy, or make her want to eat strange foods.

Growing in the womb

In the womb, the fertilized egg doubles to make two cells. These cells double to make four cells. This happens again and again, and the baby gets bigger and bigger. It grows a head, organs and limbs. Over nine months, one cell becomes a fully formed baby.

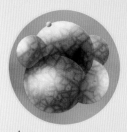

This picture shows a tiny embryo – a very small unborn baby. It is about three days old and is made up of just a few cells.

★

This embryo is about six weeks old. It has already developed a head, arms and legs.

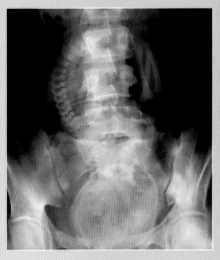

This X-ray shows a baby that's just about to be born. It has turned upside down, ready to come out of its mother's body headfirst.

Being born

When a baby is ready to be born, it usually turns upside down, and muscles around the womb squeeze it headfirst toward the vagina. Then the muscles slowly squeeze and push the baby out. This process is called labor. Some babies are born another way, in an operation called a Caesarean. Doctors cut open the womb, lift the baby out and sew the womb up again.

This is a newborn baby. Just after birth, doctors cut and clip the umbilical cord, which joins the baby to its mother inside the womb. You can see the clip in this picture.

Growing up

It takes a long time to change from a baby into an adult – up to 20 years. In this time, you grow about three times taller and 20 times heavier than when you were born. You also learn more than at any other time of your life.

Early learning

The first few years of life are when you learn the most. New babies cannot see clearly, make decisions or understand words, because they do not have a fully developed set of connections in their brains (see page 51).

However, each experience a baby has makes new connections form in its brain, allowing small children to learn things very fast. At the age of two, for example, children can memorize up to ten new words every day.

Children learn to talk, and to do all kinds of other things too, by watching and copying their parents and other people around them.

INTERNET LINK

For a link to a website where you can read more about what happens to your body during puberty, go to **www.usborne.com/quicklinks**

Getting bigger

As well as learning a lot, growing up means getting bigger. When you are growing up, your body makes millions of new cells to help your bones, muscles, skin and other body parts to grow longer and thicker.

Not all body parts grow at the same rate. For example, an adult's legs are up to five times longer than a baby's, but your head changes much less in size.

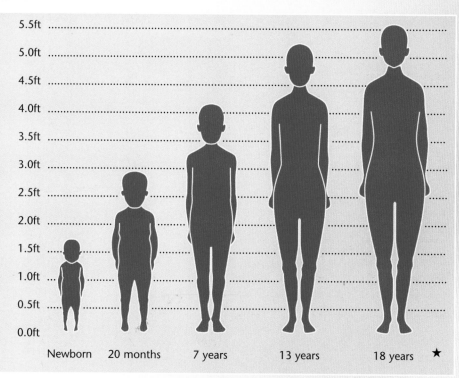

5.5ft
5.0ft
4.5ft
4.0ft
3.5ft
3.0ft
2.5ft
2.0ft
1.5ft
1.0ft
0.5ft
0.0ft

Newborn   20 months   7 years   13 years   18 years ★

Puberty

Between the ages of about 10 and 18, your body goes through puberty – a series of changes that turn you into an adult.

Boys

- grow much taller
- grow hair on face and armpits and around the sex organs
- chest, shoulders and sex organs (penis and testes) grow bigger
- voice becomes much deeper

Girls

- grow much taller
- grow breasts
- grow hair in the armpits and around the sex organs
- hips grow wider
- start having periods

The blue areas in this microscope photo are sperm starting to form inside the testes.

Ready for babies

What's the purpose of puberty? The reason people go through the changes of puberty is so that their bodies can release sperm and egg cells, which can join up to make new babies (see page 88).

This diagram shows a woman's reproductive system – the organs she uses to have a baby.

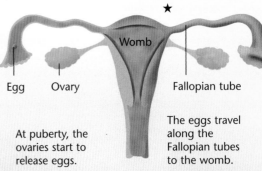

Womb

Egg   Ovary   Fallopian tube

At puberty, the ovaries start to release eggs.

The eggs travel along the Fallopian tubes to the womb.

During puberty, a boy's testes start making sperm. Girls already have all their egg cells when they are born, but at puberty, the ovaries begin releasing the eggs so that they can be used.

Periods

Since women are the ones who get pregnant, a girl's body also has to change so that it can carry a baby inside it. This is why women have periods. Every month, the inside of a woman's womb (the organ for carrying babies) gets thicker, ready to receive a fertilized egg. If no egg arrives, the womb lining breaks down into blood and comes out of the woman's vagina. This is called having a period.

Puberty makes you grow much taller in just a few years. This 15-year-old girl is now a lot taller than her ten-year-old sister.

Hormones

Your body changes throughout your life as you grow bigger, turn into an adult, and grow old. It changes from one minute to the next as well – for example, your heart beats faster when you're scared. But what makes these changes happen? The answer is hormones.

What are hormones?

Hormones are a type of chemical. They act as signals that tell different parts of your body what to do. Your body can make over 20 hormones, each with a different job. For example, growth hormones make you grow bigger as you get older, and melatonin helps you go to sleep.

Hormone glands

Hormones come from glands. A gland is a small organ that releases a particular chemical. You have many types of glands – for example, sweat glands release sweat. The glands that release hormones are called endocrine glands.

This diagram shows where your main endocrine glands are.

In scary situations, your body releases a hormone called adrenaline. It makes your heart beat faster so that you can run away.

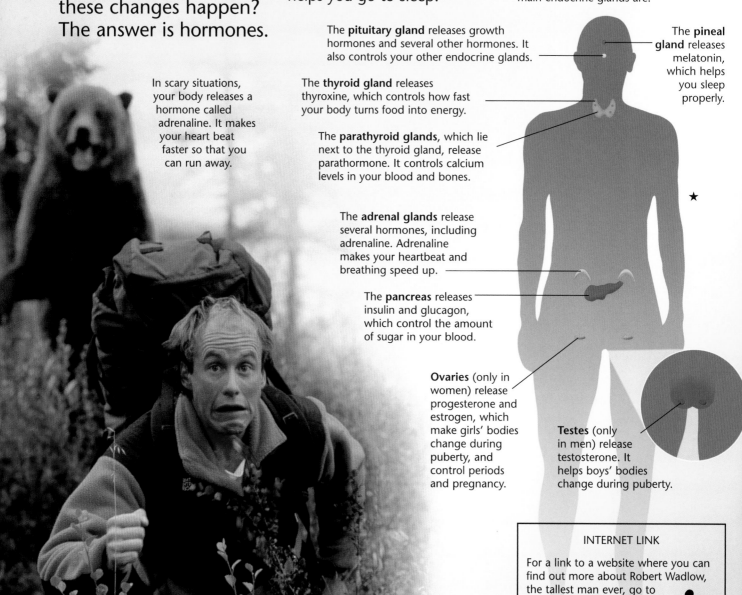

The **pituitary gland** releases growth hormones and several other hormones. It also controls your other endocrine glands.

The **thyroid gland** releases thyroxine, which controls how fast your body turns food into energy.

The **parathyroid glands**, which lie next to the thyroid gland, release parathormone. It controls calcium levels in your blood and bones.

The **adrenal glands** release several hormones, including adrenaline. Adrenaline makes your heartbeat and breathing speed up.

The **pancreas** releases insulin and glucagon, which control the amount of sugar in your blood.

Ovaries (only in women) release progesterone and estrogen, which make girls' bodies change during puberty, and control periods and pregnancy.

The **pineal gland** releases melatonin, which helps you sleep properly.

Testes (only in men) release testosterone. It helps boys' bodies change during puberty.

INTERNET LINK

For a link to a website where you can find out more about Robert Wadlow, the tallest man ever, go to **www.usborne.com/quicklinks**

Tall and small

Sometimes, if the pituitary gland doesn't work properly, the body can release too much or too little growth hormone as a person grows up. This can lead to some people being unusually short, while others grow unusually tall. The world's tallest ever man, Robert Wadlow, grew to 8ft, 11in tall, because of his overactive pituitary gland.

This picture shows two men who have grown to unusual heights because of diseases of the hormone glands. The woman in the picture is of normal height.

Feeling funny

Hormones can affect the way you feel – especially the strong hormones that make your body change during puberty and pregnancy.

For example, teenage boys' bodies make a lot of testosterone. It helps them grow taller, develop a deeper voice and grow facial hair. However, testosterone can also make people feel angry and aggressive. Extra hormones may explain why teenagers often have strong emotions and bad moods.

How hormones work

An endocrine gland works by releasing a hormone into your bloodstream. Your blood carries the hormone around your body until it reaches its "target organ" – the body part that needs it. For example, adrenaline comes from the adrenal glands near your kidneys, but its main target organ is your heart. Some hormones work in pairs to keep a body system in balance. You can see below how this works.

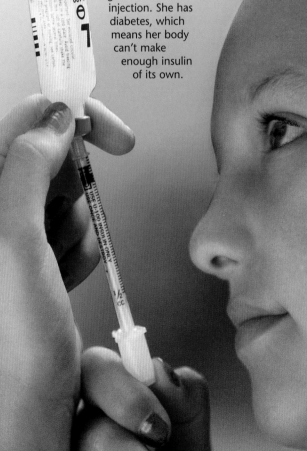

This girl is preparing to give herself an insulin injection. She has diabetes, which means her body can't make enough insulin of its own.

This diagram shows how the hormones insulin and glucagon work together to control your blood sugar.

 Too much blood sugar – pancreas releases more insulin.

 Not enough blood sugar – pancreas releases more glucagon.

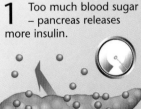

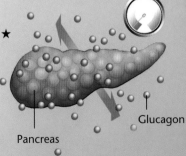

Insulin

Pancreas

Glucagon

Pancreas

2 Blood sugar level drops.

2 Blood sugar level rises.

Getting old

Everyone grows old and eventually dies. But why? The answers are partly to do with hormones, and partly to do with instructions stored in the DNA inside our cells. Our bodies also grow old because they wear out, through being used for a whole lifetime.

Hormone loss

As you grow older, your body makes less and less of some types of hormones. Since hormones help to keep your body healthy, this means that you get weaker and less healthy as time goes on.

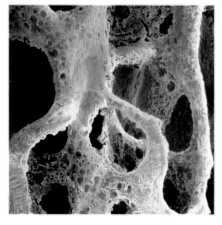

This elderly man has graying hair and deep wrinkles on his forehead and around his eyes.

This is a microscope photo of the inside of a bone affected by osteoporosis. This makes bones weaker and more brittle as you get older.

For example, your bones break more easily when you are old. As people get older, especially women, their bodies make less of the hormone estrogen. This can cause osteoporosis, which makes bones thinner and weaker.

Wearing out

Another reason you get old is that your body parts wear out. Your joints get worn down, so it's painful to walk. The lenses in your eyes grow stiffer, so it's hard to focus on things. Some older people go deaf, because their eardrums are less springy.

The blood vessels in your body also grow weaker, so they can't squeeze blood around your body very well. Your organs and muscles don't get very much oxygen, so they gradually slow down and stop working so well.

Most people's teeth start to wear out as they get older. Some people end up having their teeth taken out, and wearing false ones like these instead.

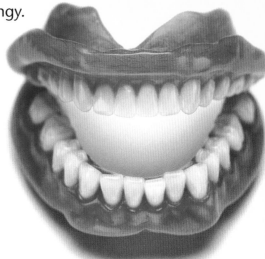

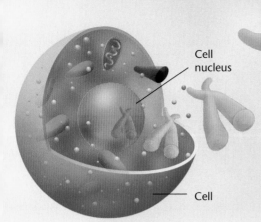

Cell nucleus

Cell

Chromosome

Each chromosome is made of a long, coiled-up strand of DNA.

Each cell has a number of chromosomes inside its nucleus. They are made of DNA and hold instructions that make your body work.

★

Skin and hair

Over time, skin gets stretched and creased as you move, talk, laugh and frown. Gravity, wind and sunshine also wear skin out. Eventually, it starts to sag and crease into bags and wrinkles. Hair color comes from a chemical called melanin, which is made by your hair roots. As you get older, they lose the ability to make melanin and your hair turns white.

INTERNET LINK

For a link to a website where you can find out why people shrink as they get older, go to www.usborne.com/quicklinks

Telomere time bomb

Even your individual cells are destined to slow down and stop. Each of the chromosomes (see page 14) inside your cells has an end section called a telomere. You keep living because your cells are always dividing to make new cells to replace old, dead ones. But each time a cell divides, its telomeres get shorter. When they reach a certain length, the cell cannot divide anymore, so old cells are no longer replaced.

A telomere is the end section of a chromosome. Each time a cell divides and its chromosomes are copied, the telomeres get shorter.

Telomere

Dying

When you die, all your body systems shut down. Your heart stops, so blood stops being pumped around your body. You stop breathing, so your cells receive no oxygen, and your organs can no longer work.

After a while, dead bodies rot away as bacteria and parasites start to feed on them. The bones are left behind, because they are mainly made of minerals and don't rot. This is why archaeologists still find the skeletons of people who lived hundreds or even thousands of years ago.

These bones belonging to a Neanderthal man, a type of early human, were found in France in 1908. The Neanderthals lived from 130,000 to 30,000 years ago.

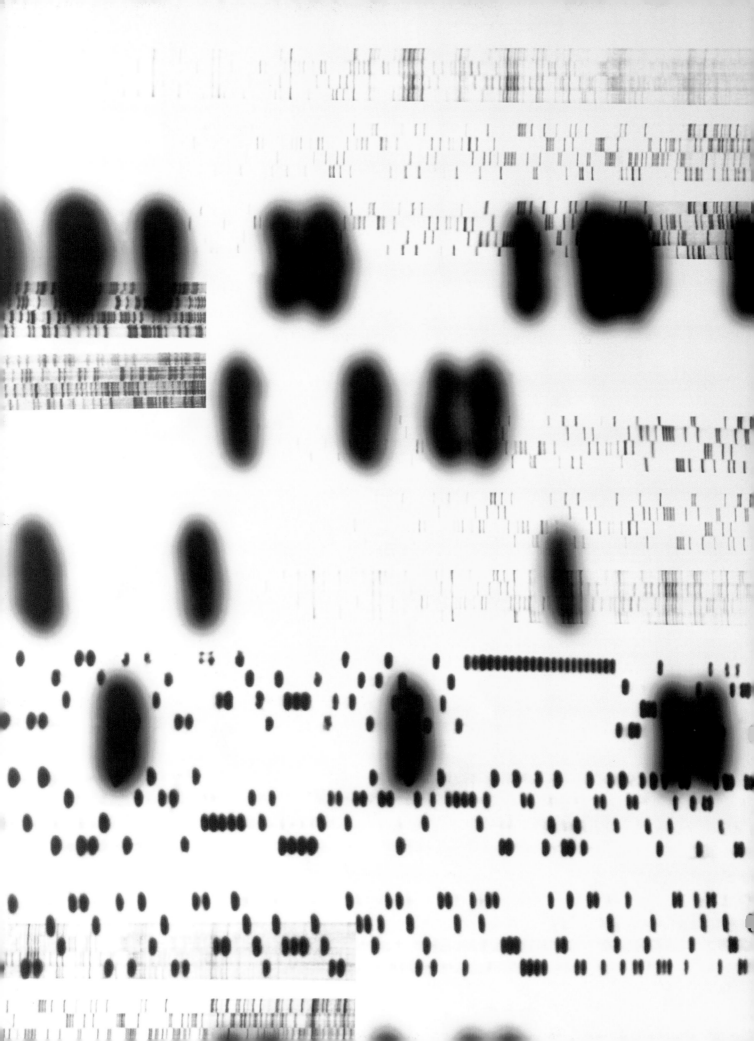

Facts and Figures

This section of the book is full of amazing facts and figures, world records, and other useful information. It includes a guide to the most important discoveries in the history of medicine and body science, and biographies of some of the great scientists who made them. It also contains a glossary explaining more than 200 body science words and phrases, and two pages of activities and experiments for you to try.

These patterns are DNA autoradiograms, which represent the sequences of chemicals in sections of human DNA. Autoradiograms are used to compare DNA samples from different people.

Facts, figures and records

These two pages list some amazing facts, figures and world records to do with the incredible human body.

Facts and figures

Body building blocks
• The average adult human body contains between 50 trillion and 100 trillion cells.

• There are about 200 different kinds of human cells.

• More than two trillion of your body cells die every day and have to be replaced by new ones.

• The bone marrow inside your bones makes about 1.2 million new red blood cells every second.

• When brain cells die, they are usually not replaced. Up to 10,000 of them die every day.

• A typical human cell is about ten microns across – or approximately 0.0004 of an inch.

• Humans have 46 chromosomes inside the nucleus of most of their cells. Chromosomes are long, thin molecules of the chemical DNA.

• An average chromosome contains about 1,300 genes.

• The complete human genome (set of human genes) contains about 30,000 genes.

• An average adult human body contains about 80 pints of water, making up around 70% of its total weight.

Muscles and bones
• An adult has 206 bones. A newborn baby has up to 270 bones, but some of them fuse together as it grows into an adult.

• The smallest bone in the body is the stapes or stirrup bone in the ear. It's less than 0.15 of an inch long.

• The biggest, heaviest and longest bone in the human body is the femur (thighbone). In some men, it can grow to be up to 2ft long.

• The adult human body has 32 teeth. Before growing adult teeth, children grow a first set of 20 smaller teeth called milk teeth.

• The human body contains about 650 skeletal muscles (the muscles that are attached to your bones).

• The biggest muscle in the body is the gluteus maximus. You have one in each buttock.

Skin, hair and nails
• A typical human body has five million hair follicles. One hair can grow out of each follicle.

• An average person has about 100,000 hair follicles on their head.

• Hair grows at a rate of about 0.4 of an inch per month.

• The human body has three million sweat pores and releases more than a pint of sweat a day.

• You shed about 40 million dead skin cells every day. In a lifetime, you'll shed up to 45 pounds of skin.

• Fingernails grow at a rate of about 0.1 of an inch per month.

The brain and the senses
• Your brain makes up only 2% of your body weight, but uses up 20% of your energy.

• The human brain can make 20 million billion calculations per second, making it faster than any computer in the world.

• A typical human can detect about 4,000 different smells and over 10,000 different colors.

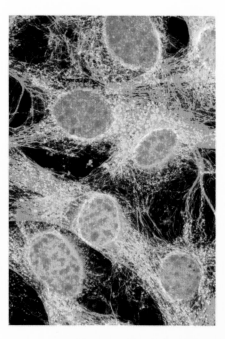

This microscope picture shows the cells that make up connective tissue, which holds body parts and organs together.

Breathing and circulation
• If all the blood vessels in one human body were stretched out, they would be about 60,000 miles long – long enough to reach twice around the Earth.

• An average adult's heart beats about 75 times per minute. That's 4,500 beats an hour, or 108,000 beats a day. In a lifetime, a heart beats about 3 billion times.

Eating and drinking
• Your mouth releases about three cups of saliva a day.

• Food takes about three days to pass through your digestive system.

• There are more bacteria living inside one person's intestines than there are human beings on Earth.

Body changes
• Humans take up to 20 years to grow into adults – much longer than most other animals.

• The average number of children born to women around the world is 2.8 each.

World records

Tallest man – Robert Wadlow from the USA was the tallest man ever. He was born in 1918 and died in 1940, aged 22. He grew to be 8ft 11in tall.

Tallest woman – Zeng Jinlian of China is thought to be the tallest woman ever. She lived from 1964 to 1982 and was 8ft 1.6in when she died.

Shortest man – The shortest man ever measured is Chandra Bahadur Dangi from Reemkholi in Nepal who was born in 1939. He measured just 1ft 9.5in tall in 2012.

Shortest woman – This was Pauline Musters, an acrobat and dancer from the Netherlands, known as "Princess Pauline". She was born in 1876 and measured exactly 2ft shortly before her death in 1895.

Oldest person – There are many claims to the longest lifespan, but the oldest person for whom there are reliable records was Jeanne Calment from France. She was born in 1875 and died in 1997, at the age of 122, and she was active throughout her old age. She was still riding a bicycle at the age of 100, acted in a film at the age of 114, and released a pop record at the age of 121.

Longest hair – The record-holder for the world's longest hair is Xie Qiuping of China. When his hair was officially measured in 2004, it was 18ft 5.5in long.

Longest fingernails – The longest fingernails ever belonged to Melvin Boothe of the USA (1948 – 2009). In May 2009, the nails on both his hands measured a total of 32ft 3.8in.

Most children born to one woman – A Russian woman named Mrs. Vassilyev, who lived from 1707 to 1782, gave birth to the most children on record – 69 altogether. They included 16 sets of twins and seven sets of triplets.

Did you know?

• It's impossible to sneeze with your eyes open.

• Human blood has the same salinity (saltiness) as sea water.

• You are taller in the morning than in the evening. During the day, the cartilage in your spine squashes down by up to 0.3in because of the effect of gravity. At night, when you lie down, the cartilage expands again.

• Your nose keeps growing throughout your life.

• An average human body contains enough iron to make a nail 1in long. The body also contains small amounts of zinc, copper, nickel and aluminum.

• A typical person spends one-third of his or her life asleep.

• In your lifetime, you will probably blink your eyes about 500 million times. You spend about a year of your life with your eyes shut because you are blinking.

• A sneeze travels out of your mouth at a speed of more than 100mph.

• In one day, your blood travels a distance of about 12,000 miles as it is pumped around and around your body.

• Children have a better sense of smell than adults. It is at its most sensitive when you are about ten years old, and then gets worse the older you get.

• Everyone has unique fingerprints, even identical twins. The ridges on your fingers appear after three months in the womb.

• The enamel that covers your teeth is the hardest substance in your body.

• Human bone is stronger than concrete or steel.

• An average person has more than 1,000 dreams every year. You forget most of your dreams.

• After the age of about 30, the human body starts to shrink.

Frenchwoman Jeanne Calment, who lived to be the oldest person in the world, photographed in France in 1995 at the age of 120

Timeline

This timeline charts some of the key events in the history of body science.

c.10,000BC
People in Africa, the Americas and Europe used early forms of surgery such as trepanning (making holes in the skull).

c.2,000BC
The ancient Egyptians made remedies for ailments such as baldness and stomachaches, and studied the heart and blood vessels.

c.700BC
The Etruscans, who lived in the area that is now Italy, made false teeth out of animal teeth held together with gold.

c.400BC
Hippocrates, an ancient Greek doctor, realized that illnesses had natural causes, not magical causes as many people believed.

c.320BC
Aristotle studied animals to find out how the heart works and how babies grow in the womb.

c.300BC
Herophilus dissected human bodies and described human organs and body parts.

c.AD170
The great Greek doctor Galen, who lived in Rome, wrote over 100 works about all aspects of medicine and the human body.

c.AD200
The Hindu medical book *Susruta Samhita* listed many herbal medicines and operations.

980
The great surgeon Abu Al-Qasim Al-Zahravi wrote a 30-volume medical encyclopedia and invented many new surgical instruments.

1240
Middle Eastern doctor Ibn Al-Nafis Damishqui studied the circulatory system, the lungs and the eyes.

1490
Italian artist and scientist Leonardo da Vinci made anatomical drawings and studies of the human body.

1573
Italian anatomist Costanzo Varolio dissected human brains, and wrote a book called *De Nervis Opticis* about brain anatomy.

1628
English doctor William Harvey published his book *On the Motion of the Heart and Blood in Animals*, detailing his discoveries about how the heart and blood vessels work.

1658
Dutch scientist Jan Swammerdam became the first person to see red blood cells through a microscope, but didn't realize what they were.

1660s
Doctors developed the first blood transfusions by injecting people with blood from animals.

1677
Dutch scientist Anton van Leeuwenhoek used microscopes to to see blood cells and sperm cells.

1680
Italian scientist Giovanni Borelli studied the way the skeleton and muscles work together to make the body move.

1786
Italian doctor Luigi Galvani saw that electricity could make dead animals twitch. From this he realized that the body uses electrical signals to send messages along nerves.

1865
French scientist Louis Pasteur proved that some types of diseases could be spread by germs traveling through the air.

1867
English doctor Joseph Lister developed the use of antiseptic to keep wounds germ-free after operations, saving many lives.

1900
Various scientists discovered chromosomes inside cells and realized that they contained genes.

1928
Scottish scientist Alexander Fleming discovered antibiotics. In later years, these bacteria-killing drugs were to save millions of lives.

1953
US biologist James Watson and English biologist Francis Crick discovered the structure of DNA.

1967
South African doctor Christiaan Barnard performed the first heart transplant.

2001
Scientists announced that they had made the first map of the human genome, the complete sequence of human genes.

In this 1804 illustration, a doctor treats a patient by "bloodletting" – draining blood from the body. Bloodletting was used all the way up until the 20th century, but experts now believe it was not effective.

Who's who

This who's who lists some of the great scientists, thinkers and writers who have contributed to our knowledge and understanding of the human body.

This 19th-century illustration shows Louis Pasteur vaccinating patients to protect them against diseases carried by germs.

Abu Al-Qasim Al-Zahravi (936-1013) Famous surgeon and royal doctor to the king of Spain. He invented many medical instruments and new surgical techniques.

Aristotle (384-322BC) Ancient Greek who studied many subjects, including the human body. He used his studies of animals to guess how the human body worked.

Christiaan Barnard (1922-2001) South African doctor and pioneer of open heart surgery. In 1967, after experimenting on dogs, he carried out the first human heart transplant on a 55-year-old patient named Louis Washkansky.

Giovanni Borelli (1608-1697) Italian scientist who applied the laws of physics to the human body in order to understand the relationship between muscles, bones and human movement.

Francis Crick (1916-2004) English biologist who, along with James Watson, discovered the structure of DNA in 1953. He was awarded a Nobel Prize in 1962.

Alexander Fleming (1881-1955) Scottish scientist who accidentally discovered penicillin, a mold containing a type of antibiotic, when it grew on some bacteria in his lab. He was given a Nobel Prize in 1945, after other scientists developed antibiotics for medical use.

Rosalind Franklin (1920-1958) English scientist who studied DNA and helped to uncover its structure.

Galen (Claudius Galenus) (AD131-201) Ancient Greek who was a royal doctor to five Roman emperors. He studied all aspects of medicine, and his ideas greatly influenced medicine for the next 1,500 years.

Luigi Galvani (1737-1798) Italian scientist and surgeon who discovered that nerve impulses are partly electrical, after an electrical current caused a dead frog's leg he was dissecting to move by itself.

William Harvey (1578-1657) English royal doctor who studied the circulatory system. He proved that the heart was a pump that circulated blood around the body.

Herophilus (c.335-280BC) Ancient Greek scientist who dissected bodies to find out about internal organs. He made important discoveries about the brain, liver and other organs.

Hippocrates (c.460-370BC) Ancient Greek doctor, often called the father of medicine. He argued that diseases had natural causes and developed many medical theories.

Ibn Al-Nafis Damishqui (1213-1288) Doctor who ran a hospital in Cairo, Egypt. He developed a theory of the circulation of the blood that was later proved by William Harvey.

Edward Jenner (1749-1823) English doctor who developed the use of vaccination to prevent disease.

Anton van Leeuwenhoek (1632-1723) Dutch amateur microscope scientist who discovered several types of body cells and bacteria.

Leonardo da Vinci (1452-1519) Italian artist, scientist and thinker who made detailed anatomical drawings of the human body.

Joseph Lister (1827-1912) English doctor who developed the use of antiseptic to kill germs.

Louis Pasteur (1822-1895) French scientist who proved that germs could travel through the air and cause diseases and decay.

Jan Swammerdam (1637-1680) Dutch scientist who was the first person to see red blood cells.

Costanzo Varolio (1543-1575) Italian scientist who was one of the first to dissect and study the brain.

James Watson (born 1928) US biologist who helped to discover the structure of DNA. He won a Nobel Prize in 1962.

INTERNET LINKS

For links to websites where you can read about more body scientists, go to **www.usborne.com/quicklinks**

Experiments and activities

If you'd like to be a body scientist yourself, try these easy experiments. Just use your own body as a subject, or compare results with your friends.

Take your pulse

Try taking your pulse before and after doing exercise, such as running for two minutes.

1 Push up your sleeve and hold your hand out with the palm facing you, like this. Place the first two fingers of your other hand on your wrist, just down from your thumb.

2 Press gently to feel your pulse. Then, using a stopwatch or a watch or clock with a second hand, count how many times your pulse beats in a minute. This is your pulse rate.

Test your knee reflex

Doctors sometimes test your knee reflex to make sure your nervous system is working properly. It makes your leg kick forward if your knee is tapped in a particular place.

1 Sit with your legs crossed so that one knee rests on top of the other and your foot is off the ground, like this.

2 Tap your knee sharply, just below the kneecap, with a solid object – the edge of a book works well.

3 When you hit the right spot, your foot should jerk forward automatically – even if you try to stop it.

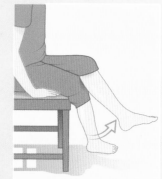

Test your reaction time

How long does it take for your brain to process what you can see and send your muscles a message to move? Find out with this simple reaction-time experiment.

1 Ask a friend to hold a ruler at the top like this, so that the low numbers are at the bottom.

2 Hold out your finger and thumb at the bottom of the ruler without touching it, just below the number 0.

3 Your friend should then let go of the ruler. Try to catch it as soon as you can when you see it start to drop.

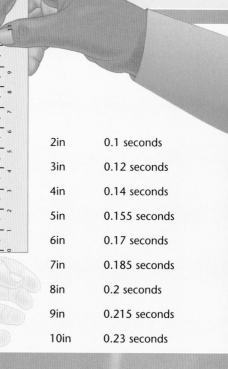

Where did your fingers grab the ruler? The chart shows your reaction time. Most people take about 0.15 seconds.

2in	0.1 seconds
3in	0.12 seconds
4in	0.14 seconds
5in	0.155 seconds
6in	0.17 seconds
7in	0.185 seconds
8in	0.2 seconds
9in	0.215 seconds
10in	0.23 seconds

Measure your lung capacity

This experiment lets you find out how much air your lungs can hold. You'll need a large plastic drink bottle with a lid, a measuring cup, a large plastic bowl, a bendable straw and a permanent marker. Before you start, try guessing who among your friends has the most lung capacity.

Measuring cup — Plastic bottle

Permanent marker

Plastic bowl

1 First, mark measurements on the bottle. Using the measuring cup, pour water into the bottle in 1-cup amounts, and mark the level each time until the bottle is full.

2 Half-fill the plastic bowl with water. Then fill the bottle with water right up to the top, so that there is no air inside it at all.

Bottle lid

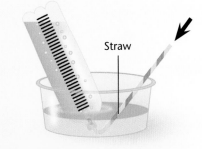

Straw

3 Put the lid on the bottle and screw it down firmly. Then hold the bottle upside down in the bowl. When the neck of the bottle is underwater, take the lid off, keeping the neck underwater all the time.

4 Push the straw into the neck of the bottle. Breathe in as deeply as you can, then blow gently into the straw until your lungs are empty. The amount of air in the bottle is your lung capacity.

How fast do your nails grow?

This experiment takes a few weeks. See if your nails grow faster than your friends', or try comparing the growth rates of fingernails and toenails.

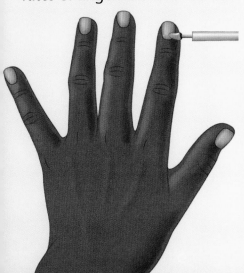

1 Paint one of your nails with nail polish, right up to where the skin starts at the base of the nail. (If you don't want to paint the whole nail, you can just paint a small area at the bottom.)

2 Once a week, measure the distance between the skin at the base of the nail, and the start of the nail polish. How much does the nail grow in a month?

Temperature tests

Do you think your body is good at guessing how hot or cold things are? To find out, try this temperature-testing experiment. It's a good idea to do this experiment in the sink or bathtub in case you spill any water.

1 Fill a large bowl with lukewarm water.

2 Now take two smaller bowls or cups. Fill one with cold water, and the other with water that's as hot as bath water.

3 Put one hand in the cold water, and the other in the hot water. Hold them there for one minute.

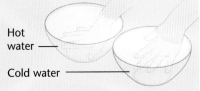

Hot water ——

Cold water ——

4 Take your hands out and plunge them both into the large bowl of lukewarm water. What can you feel?

The water probably feels very hot to one of your hands, and very cold to the other. This shows that the way you feel temperature depends on the temperature your body is already at.

INTERNET LINK

For a link to a website where you can find lots more experiments to do with the human body, go to **www.usborne.com/quicklinks**

Glossary

This glossary explains some of the words you may have seen in this book or in other books about the human body.

A

abdomen The part of the body between the chest and the hips.

Achilles tendon A large, very strong tendon that connects the calf muscle to the heel.

acupuncture A Chinese medical treatment in which needles are inserted into points on the body.

adenosine triphosphate see **ATP**.

adrenal gland A gland near the kidneys that makes adrenaline.

adrenaline A hormone that can be released to increase your heart rate and give you a short energy boost.

allergy If you have an allergy (or are allergic) to something, such as dust or pollen, your body reacts to it as if it were a dangerous germ.

alternative medicine Another name for complementary medicine.

alveoli Tiny sacs inside your lungs where oxygen passes into the blood.

amino acids The chemical building blocks that living things use to build proteins.

amputate To remove a body part such as a leg or finger.

amygdala A part of the brain that makes you feel fear and anxiety.

anesthetic A drug or gas given to patients before operations to stop them from feeling any pain.

antibiotics Medicines that can cure some illnesses by killing bacteria.

antibodies Chemicals in the body that destroy or disable germs.

aorta The biggest artery in the body, which carries blood out of the heart.

arteries Blood vessels that carry blood away from the heart toward the rest of the body.

ATP (adenosine triphosphate) A chemical that stores energy inside your muscles.

auditory nerve The nerve that carries sound signals from the ear into the brain.

B

bacteria (singular: bacterium) Tiny single-celled organisms. Some types of bacteria cause diseases, but others are harmless or even useful.

bile A green liquid released by the liver that helps your body to digest fatty food.

blood clot A lump of hardened blood. Blood often clots to make scabs over wounds, but it can also form clots inside the body.

bloodstream The flow of blood around the body.

blood vessels Tubes that carry blood around the body.

body system A group of organs and body parts that work together to do a particular job. For example, the digestive system digests food.

body tissues Groups of cells joined together to make up body parts.

bolus A ball of swallowed food.

bone marrow A soft material found inside some bones, which makes red blood cells.

bowel or bowels Another name for the intestines.

bronchi Two thick tubes that lead from the trachea into the two lungs.

bronchioles Tiny tubes inside the lungs that carry air to the alveoli.

C

cancer A disease that happens when cells reproduce too fast and grow out of control.

capillaries Tiny blood vessels that deliver oxygen and food to cells, and carry waste products away.

carbon dioxide A gas that cells make as a waste product. It is carried to the lungs to be breathed out.

cardiac muscle The type of muscle the heart is made of.

cartilage A tough, flexible material found in body parts such as the nose, ears and spine.

cell A tiny living unit. Cells make up the bodies of living things. The human body is made up of millions of cells.

central nervous system The brain and the spinal cord.

cerebellum A part of the brain that controls muscles and balance.

cerebrum The largest part of the brain. It controls many body functions and actions and is also used for thinking.

chromosome A strand of DNA found inside a cell nucleus, containing a number of genes.

chyme The soupy mixture that food turns into inside your stomach.

cilia (singular: cilium) Tiny hair-like or finger-like shapes found in various parts of the body, including the trachea and the nose.

circulation The movement of blood around and around the body.

circulatory system The organs and tubes that circulate blood around the body, including the heart and blood vessels.

clone A living thing that is an exact genetic copy of another living thing.

cochlea A spiral-shaped tube inside the ear that detects sound vibrations.

colon A name for the main part of the large intestine.

complementary medicine Unconventional medical treatments, such as acupuncture, that are used instead of or alongside conventional medicines to treat some illnesses.

conception The moment when a man's sperm cell and a woman's egg cell join together to make a fertilized egg cell that can grow into a baby.

consciousness The brain's ability to be aware of its own thoughts.

cornea A transparent covering that protects the front of the eye.

corpus callosum A bundle of nerve fibers that connects the two halves of the cerebrum.

cortex The outer part of an organ. The cerebral cortex is the outer part of the cerebrum, the part of the brain used for thinking.

cranium The part of the skull that surrounds the brain.

cytoplasm A jelly-like substance that fills most of the inside of a cell.

cytoskeleton A network of tubes that helps to give a cell its shape.

D

deoxyribonucleic acid see **DNA**.

dermis The thick, lower layer of skin underneath the surface.

diaphragm A muscle below the lungs that helps you breathe.

digestive system A set of organs and body parts that breaks down food, extracts useful chemicals from it and carries waste out of your body.

DNA (deoxyribonucleic acid) The chemical, found in cell nuclei, that makes up genes and chromosomes.

E

ear canal A tube that carries sound from the outer ear to the eardrum.

eardrum A thin sheet of tissue inside the ear, which vibrates when it is hit by sound waves.

egg cell A female reproductive cell that can join with a man's sperm cell to make a fertilized egg cell, which can grow into a baby.

embryo A fertilized egg in the early stages of growing into a baby.

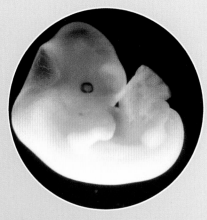

This five-week-old human embryo is starting to develop a head and eyes.

enamel The hard, white substance that forms the surface of a tooth.

endocrine system A set of glands that releases hormones to control the way your body works.

endoplasmic reticulum A set of channels that transports various substances around inside a cell.

epidermis Outer layer of the skin.

epiglottis A flap of muscle in the throat that closes when you swallow, to stop food from entering the lungs.

esophagus The tube that carries food from the throat to the stomach.

F

Fallopian tubes Tubes in a woman's body that carry egg cells from the ovaries to the womb.

fertilize An egg cell is fertilized when it fuses with a sperm cell, making a new cell that can grow into a baby.

fever A high body temperature.

fiber The tough parts of food that cannot be digested. Nerve and muscle cells can also be called fibers.

G

gall bladder An organ that stores **bile** until it is needed.

gastric juices Acidic liquids in the stomach that help to dissolve food.

gastric pits Tiny hollows in the lining of the stomach where gastric juices are released.

gene A section of DNA that acts as a code, telling cells how to make a particular body protein.

genome A complete set of genes. For example, the human genome is the complete set of all the genes needed to make a human being.

germ A microorganism, such as a bacterium or virus, that causes disease.

glands Small organs that release chemicals that help the body work.

Golgi complex A unit inside a cell that stores spare proteins and sends them to wherever they are needed.

H

hair follicles The tiny tubes in your skin that hairs grow out of.

heart attack A sudden shortage of blood to the heart, usually caused by a blockage in the blood vessels supplying the heart.

hippocampus A part of the brain that helps to process experiences.

homeopathy A complementary medical treatment which is said to work by using tiny doses of medicine to stimulate the body to cure itself.

hormones Chemicals that the body releases into the bloodstream to control some body functions.

hypothalamus A part of the brain that controls hormones and regulates your body temperature.

I

immune system A set of organs and body parts that fights germs or dirt that get into the body.

insulin A hormone that controls the way your body digests sugar.

intestines Long tubes that form part of your digestive system. There are two types: the small intestine and the large intestine.

involuntary muscles Muscles that move automatically, without you having to think about them.

iris The colored, ring-shaped part of the eye. It contains muscles which control the size of the pupil.

J

joint Any point where two bones in the skeleton are linked together.

K

kidney An organ that filters waste chemicals from the blood and controls the amount of water in the body. Most people have two kidneys.

L

large intestine A thick tube that collects and dries out waste that has passed through the digestive system.

larynx The part of the throat that contains the vocal cords, which you use for speaking.

lens A transparent disc inside the eye that directs light at the retina.

ligament A tough, stretchy band that holds bones together at a joint.

limb An arm or a leg.

liver A large organ that makes bile, stores useful chemicals and does many other jobs for the body.

lymph Surplus liquid that seeps out of blood vessels and is carried away by the lymph vessels.

lymphatic system A network of lymph vessels and lymph nodes that fights disease and drains excess liquid from your cells.

lymph node A bean-shaped lump in a lymph vessel. Lymph nodes contain white blood cells that fight diseases by killing germs.

lysosome A unit inside a cell that breaks down and reuses old proteins.

M

malaria A serious disease carried by some types of mosquitoes.

malnutrition An illness caused by a poor diet or a lack of food.

melanin A dark pigment which gives skin and hair a brown color.

membrane A thin film or sheet of body tissue, such as the eardrum.

meninges Protective membranes that surround the brain.

minerals Natural, non-living materials. Some minerals, such as iron and calcium compounds, are found in food and used by the body.

mitochondria (singular: mitochondrion) Power units in a cell. They combine food with oxygen to provide energy for the cell.

mucus A slimy substance made in some parts of the body, such as the nose and stomach.

muscular system The set of muscles that makes your body move.

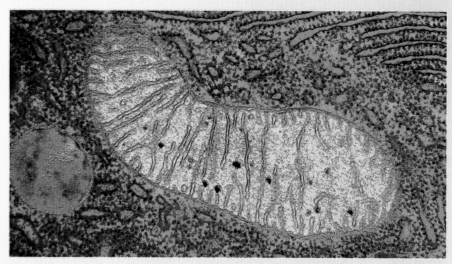

A microscope photo of a mitochondrion inside a cell, 25,000 times bigger than life-size.

N

nail bed The flesh that lies under a fingernail or toenail.

nail root The area a fingernail or toenail grows from.

nephrons Tiny filters in the kidneys that filter waste out of your blood.

nerves Bundles of nerve fibers that carry messages. They lead to and from the brain and spinal cord and into the rest of the body.

nervous system The nerves, brain and spinal cord, which control and carry messages around your body.

neuron A nerve cell, one of the cells that make up the nervous system, including the brain. Neurons are also called neurones.

nucleus (plural: nuclei) A cell's control unit. The nucleus contains genes that tell the cell how to work. Some cells, such as red blood cells, do not have a nucleus.

O

obese Extremely fat.

optic nerve A bundle of neurons that carries signals from the eye into the brain.

organ A body part that does a job for the rest of the body, such as the heart, brain or stomach.

organelles Tiny "mini-organs," such as ribosomes and mitochondria, that do different jobs inside a cell.

ovary An organ found only in women. It makes egg cells and releases female hormones.

oxygen A colorless gas found in the air. Humans need to take in oxygen to make their bodies work.

P

pancreas An organ that makes hormones and digestive juices.

papilla (plural: papillae) One of the tiny bumps on the tongue, many of which contain taste buds.

particle A very small piece or part of something.

pelvis A large, basin-shaped part of the skeleton that forms the hips. The leg bones are attached to it.

penis An organ found only in men. It is used to pass sperm into a woman's body, and to release urine.

periosteum The thin outer covering of a bone.

peristalsis A squeezing action that moves in waves to push food or liquid along inside a tube, such as the small intestine.

pharynx The part of the throat that is used for breathing and swallowing.

pinna (plural: pinnae) The outer, visible part of the ear.

pituitary gland A gland in the brain that makes growth hormones. It also controls the endocrine system.

placebo A "pretend" medicine that contains no real medicine. Drugs are often tested by comparing their effects to a placebo.

plasma A pale yellow liquid that is one of the main ingredients of blood.

platelet A type of cell fragment found in blood, and used by the body to make blood clots.

pores Tiny holes in the skin through which sweat escapes.

proprioception A body function that tells your brain where all your body parts are.

protein A type of natural substance found in living things. Cells have to make many different proteins to keep your body working.

protozoan (plural: protozoa) A tiny animal. Some protozoa are germs and cause diseases.

puberty The stage of development, between the ages of about ten and 18, when a child becomes an adult.

pulmonary artery A large artery that carries blood from the heart to the lungs.

pulmonary veins Veins that carry blood from the lungs to the heart.

pupil The round opening in the middle of the eye that lets light in.

R

rash An area of spots or sore, irritated skin.

rectum The end of the large intestine, where lumps of waste are held until you go to the toilet.

red blood cells Disc-shaped cells that carry oxygen around the body.

reflex An involuntary reaction to something, such as moving your hand away from something hot.

reproductive system The parts of the body used for reproduction (making babies).

respiratory system The set of organs that allows you to breathe in oxygen and breathe out waste gases.

retina A layer of cells at the back of the eye that detects light patterns and sends signals to the brain.

ribosome A unit inside a cell that reads instructions from genes and uses them to make new proteins.

S

salinity The percentage of salt that a substance contains.

saliva A liquid released into the mouth to dissolve food and make it easier to swallow. Also called spit.

scalp The layer of skin that covers the skull, which the hair on your head grows out of.

scalpel A sharp, knife-like tool used to cut into the body during surgery.

sebum An oily substance released by the skin to keep skin and hair soft and stop them from drying out.

sexual intercourse Also called sex, this happens when a man's penis fits into a woman's vagina so that male and female reproductive cells can join together to make a baby.

skeletal muscles Muscles that are connected to the skeleton.

skeletal system The framework of bones and joints that gives the body its shape, protects its internal organs and allows it to move.

small intestine A long tube that forms part of the digestive system. It absorbs chemicals from food and passes them into the bloodstream.

smooth muscle A type of involuntary muscle found inside the body, which causes movement in internal organs such as the stomach.

sperm A male reproductive cell that can combine with a woman's egg cell to make a fertilized egg cell that can grow into a baby.

sphincter A circular muscle which can squeeze tight to close a tube. For example the pyloric sphincter can close the passage between the stomach and the small intestine.

spinal cord Part of the central nervous system that runs from the brain down the spine and links the brain to nerves all over the body.

spine The column of 33 bones, called vertebrae, which forms the central part of the skeleton. The head, ribs and pelvis are all connected to it. It is sometimes called the backbone.

spongy bone A strong, light type of bone that has a hollow, honeycomb structure.

stomach A strong, stretchy bag that receives chewed food from the esophagus. The stomach breaks food down into liquid by squeezing it and dissolving it with acids.

surgery Medical treatment that involves cutting open the body in order to reach the internal organs or tissues. Also called an operation.

synovial fluid A thick fluid inside a joint that stops bones from scraping and grinding against each other.

T

tendon A kind of tough string that attaches a muscle to a bone.

testes Organs found only in men. They make sperm cells and release male hormones.

thalamus Part of the brain that sorts out signals entering the brain, then sends them to other areas of the brain for processing.

thyroid gland A gland found in the throat. It makes hormones that control how fast your body turns food into energy.

trachea A tube that connects the throat to the lungs and is used for breathing. It is sometimes known as the windpipe.

trepanning Cutting a hole in someone's skull while they are still alive. This was one of the earliest forms of surgery, and may have been intended to drive out evil spirits.

tuberculosis A serious disease caused by bacteria infecting the lungs, or sometimes bones or other body parts and causing them to rot.

tumor A growth caused by cells growing and dividing too fast. Some tumors are cancerous, or "malignant." Those which are not are called "benign" tumors.

U

umbilical cord A tube that connects a baby growing in the womb to its mother's body.

ureter A tube that carries urine from the kidneys to the bladder.

urethra A tube leading out of the bladder, through which urine is released when you go to the toilet.

urinary system A set of organs that controls the amount of water in the body. It includes the kidneys, bladder and urethra.

urine A waste liquid made by the kidneys from water and waste chemicals.

uterus Another name for the womb.

V

vaccination A way of protecting against a disease by using a stimulus, such as a weakened germ, to help the body to make disease antibodies.

vagina A tube that connects a woman's womb to the outside of her body. During sexual intercourse, sperm cells enter a woman's body through the vagina. When a woman gives birth, the baby is pushed out of her body through the vagina.

valve A flap of tissue that allows a liquid, such as blood, to flow in one direction but stops it from flowing back the other way. There are valves in the heart and in the veins.

veins Blood vessels that carry blood toward the heart from the rest of the body.

venae cavae Two very large veins that carry blood into the heart to be pumped to the lungs.

vertebrae (singular: vertebra) The 33 interlocking, disc-shaped bones that make up the spine or backbone.

villi (singular: villus) Tiny, finger-like shapes covering the lining of the small intestine. They soak up food chemicals and pass them into the bloodstream.

virus A type of very small germ that can spread diseases. A virus works by invading a cell and forcing it to make more copies of the virus.

visual cortex The part of the brain that processes visual images.

vitreous humor A stiff, clear, jelly-like substance that fills the eyeball and helps it to keep its shape.

vocal cords Two stretchy bands in the larynx, which vibrate to make a sound when you speak.

voice box A name for the larynx.

W

white blood cells Blood cells which help your body fight diseases by killing germs.

windpipe see **trachea**.

womb A strong, stretchy organ in women. When a woman is pregnant, the baby grows inside her womb. It stretches as the baby gets bigger.

Index

In this index, page numbers in **bold type** show where to find the main explanation of a word or topic.

Acknowledgements

The publishers are grateful to the following for permission to reproduce material:
Cover (human skeleton) Alfred Pasieka/Science Photo Library (SPL); Blood cells © SPL; Endpapers (white blood cells) Dr. Gopal Murti/SPL; p1 (blood vessels) Susumu Nishinaga/SPL; pp2-3 (skeleton) Alfred Pasieka/SPL; p4 (embryo) Dr. Yorgos Nikas/SPL; p5 (chest X-ray) Gusto/SPL; p6 (chromosome set) CNRI/SPL; pp6-7 (chromosomes) Biophoto Associates/SPL; p8 (girl) Thinkstock/Getty Images; p8 (blood cells) SPL; p10 (head) Gandee Vassan/Getty Images; p11 (lymphocyte) SPL; p12 (diatom) SPL; p12 (fat cells) Prof. P. Motta/Dept. of Anatomy/University "La Sapienza", Rome/SPL; p15 (DNA autoradiogram) Colin Cuthbert/SPL; p15 (family) Mark Anderson/Rubberball/Alamy; p15 (sheep) © PHOTOTAKE Inc./Alamy; pp16-17 (spongy bone) SPL; p18 (skeleton) Alfred Pasieka/SPL; p18 (stapes) CNRI/SPL; p19 (spongy bone) Prof. P. Motta/Dept. of Anatomy/University "La Sapienza", Rome/SPL; p19 (archaeologist) © Richard T. Nowitz/CORBIS; p20 (skeleton) John Daugherty/SPL; p21 (artificial hip) Tek Image/SPL; p21 (finger X-ray) Dept. of Clinical Radiology, Salisbury District Hospital/SPL; p21 (finger photo) Dr. P. Marazzi/SPL; p21 (contortionist) © Bob Krist/CORBIS; p22 (muscles) John Daugherty/SPL; p23 (athlete) © Kevin Dodge/CORBIS; p23 (astronaut) © CORBIS; p24 (nerves and muscle) Don Fawcett/SPL; p25 (strongman) © Bettman/CORBIS; p25 (boy) © Royalty-Free/CORBIS; p26 (smooth muscle) SPL; p26 (heart) James King-Holmes/SPL; p27 (eye) Alfred Pasieka/SPL; p27 (trumpeter) SW Productions/Getty Images; p28 (doctor & baby) Phototake/Robert Harding; p28 (water fight) Sean Murphy/Getty Images; p29 (sweat) Richard Wehr/Custom Medical Stock Photo/SPL; p30 (skin surface) SPL; p31 (swimmer) Dan Burton/Imagestate/Alamy; p31 (fingerprint) Stephen Moncrieff; p32 (kids) Jorn Georg Tomter/Getty Images; p33 (artificial skin) J. C. Revy/SPL; p33 (sunbather) Dr. Arthur Tucker/SPL; p33 (blood cells) Susumu Nishinaga/SPL; p34 (hairs) Eye of Science/SPL; p34 (scalp cross-section) John Durham/SPL; p35 (long fingernails) Jagdish Agarwal/Stock Connection, Inc./Alamy; pp36-37 (brain cells) Nancy Kedersha/UCLA/SPL; p38 (skull X-ray) Mehau Kulyk/SPL; p38 (brain in jar) © Royalty-Free/CORBIS; p39 (brain scan) Alfred Pasieka/SPL; p39 (cortex) Volker Steiger/SPL; p39 (beheading) © Archivo Iconografico, S.A./CORBIS; p41 (neurons) CNRI/SPL; p43 (biker) © Roy Morsch/CORBIS; p43 (colourblindness test) © Isshin-kai Foundation; p43 (rod & cone cells) Omikron/SPL; pp44-45 (cochlea hairs) Susumu Nishinaga/SPL; p45 (ear syringing) Hattie Young/SPL; p45 (sound waves) Mehau Kulyk/SPL; p45 (stilt dancers) © Charles & Josette Lenars/CORBIS; p46 (cell & cilia) Prof. P. Motta/Dept. of Anatomy/University "La Sapienza", Rome/SPL; p46 (skunk) © Tim Davis/CORBIS; p47 (papillae) SPL; p47 (boy) Eye-Wire/Getty Images; p48 (brain) Montreal Neuro. Institute/McGill University/CNRI/SPL; p48 (athlete) © Ng Han Guan/AP/Press Association Images; p49 (Hindu) © Michael S. Yamashita/CORBIS; p49 (hand X-ray) Zephyr/SPL; p50 (brain) Wellcome Dept. of Cognitive Neurology/SPL; p50 (experiment) age fotostock/David Riecks; p51 (crowd) Stuart McClymont/Getty Images; p51 (robot) Peter Menzel/SPL; p52 (hand) Stephen Moncrieff; p53 (blood vessel) SPL; p55 (vocal cords) CNRI/SPL; p55 (child) Frederic Cresseaux/Getty Images; p56 (cilia) Dr. G. Moscoso/SPL; p57 (lung arteries) SPL; p57 (smoker's lung) James Stevenson/SPL; p58 (heart muscle) SPL; p59 (heart X-ray) SPL; p59 (fatty artery) GJLP/SPL; p60 (body's blood vessels) Sheila Terry/SPL; p61 (pulse) Faye Norman/SPL; p61 (capillary) SPL; p62 (blood sample) Mauro Fermariello/SPL; p62 (blood cells) SPL; p63 (clotting) SPL; p63 (blood bag) Tek Image/SPL; p64 (lymph node) SPL; p64 (doctor & child) Simon Fraser/SPL; p65 (gastric pit) Pr. S. Cinti/CNRI/SPL; p66 (girl) Julie Toy/Imagebank/Getty Images; p67 (drip bag) Jim Oliver/Peter Arnold Inc./SPL; p67 (X-ray) SPL; p68 (gastric pit) Pr. S. Cinti/CNRI/SPL; p68 (cartoon) Library of Congress, USA; p69 (fairground ride) Chad Slattery/Getty Images; p69 (stomach X-ray) Zephyr/SPL; p70 (villi) SPL; p70 (small intestine) Manfred Kage/SPL; p71 (obesity) Gusto/SPL; p71 (avocado) © Lois Ellen Frank/CORBIS; p72 (large intestine) CNRI/SPL; p72 (*E. coli*) E. Gray/SPL; p73 (donor kidney) Will & Deni McIntyre/SPL; pp74-75 (*Salmonella* bacteria) BSIP/SPL; p76 (lung X-ray) Simon Fraser/SPL; p76 (swimmers) © Dan Burton Photo/Alamy; p77 (bacteria) Dr. Linda Stannard, UCT/SPL; p77 (researcher) © William Whitehurst/CORBIS; p78 (viruses) Eye of Science/SPL; pp78-79 (cancer cell) SPL; p79 (sneeze) Dr. Gary Settles/SPL; p80 (baby) © Mark L. Stephenson/CORBIS; pp80-81 (white blood cell) Biology Media/SPL; p81 (mosquito) Martin Dohrn/SPL; p81 (vaccination) © CORBIS; p82 (pills) Luca DiCecco/Alamy; p82 (protozoa) Volker Steger/Christian Bardele/SPL; p83 (tobacco) George Bernard/SPL; p83 (helmet) © Roger Ressmeyer/CORBIS; pp84-85 (operation) International Stock/Robert Harding; p85 (tools) © LWA-JDC/CORBIS; p85 (scar) Dr. P. Marazzi/SPL; p85 (skull) National Museum, Denmark/Munoz-Yague/SPL; p86 (acupuncture head) age fotostock/Garry Gay; p86 (burning moxa) Damien Lovegrove/SPL; p86 (rhubarb root) TH Foto-Werbung/SPL; p87 (pituitary gland) Profs. P. M. Motta & S. Correr/SPL; p88 (egg & sperm) Prof. P. M. Motta et al./SPL; p88 (egg on pipette) Richard Rawlins/Custom Medical Stock Photo/SPL; p89 (baby X-ray) Mehau Kulyk/SPL; p89 (newborn baby) © Tom Galliher/CORBIS; p90 (baby on phone) © Jim Cummins/CORBIS; p91 (sperm forming) CNRI/SPL; p91 (girls) Olivier Ribardiere/Getty Images; p92 (scary bear) © Galen Rowell/CORBIS; p93 (tall & small) SPL; p93 (diabetic girl) © Royalty-Free/CORBIS; p94 (osteoporosis) Prof. P. Motta/Dept. of Anatomy/University "La Sapienza", Rome/SPL; p94 (old man) © Don Mason/CORBIS; p94 (false teeth) Gusto/SPL; p95 (bones) John Reader/SPL; pp96-97 (DNA autoradiogram) Alfred Pasieka/SPL; p98 (cells) Dr. Gopal Murti/SPL; p99 (Jeanne Calment) © Parrot Pascal/CORBIS SYGMA; p100 (blood-letting) © Historical Picture Archive/CORBIS; p101 (Pasteur) © Bettman/CORBIS; p105 (embryo) Profs. P. M. Motta & S. Makabe/SPL; p106 (mitochondrion) Bill Longcore/SPL.

Every effort has been made to trace and acknowledge ownership of copyright. If any rights have been omitted, the publishers offer to rectify this in any subsequent editions following notification.

Artwork for pp102-103 by John Woodcock • Cover design by Dianne Doñaque and Tom Lalonde • Picture research by Ruth King • Proofreading and Internet research by Claire Masset • Additional digital image manipulation by Glen Bird • Additional research by Judy Claybourne • Special thanks to Fiona Chandler

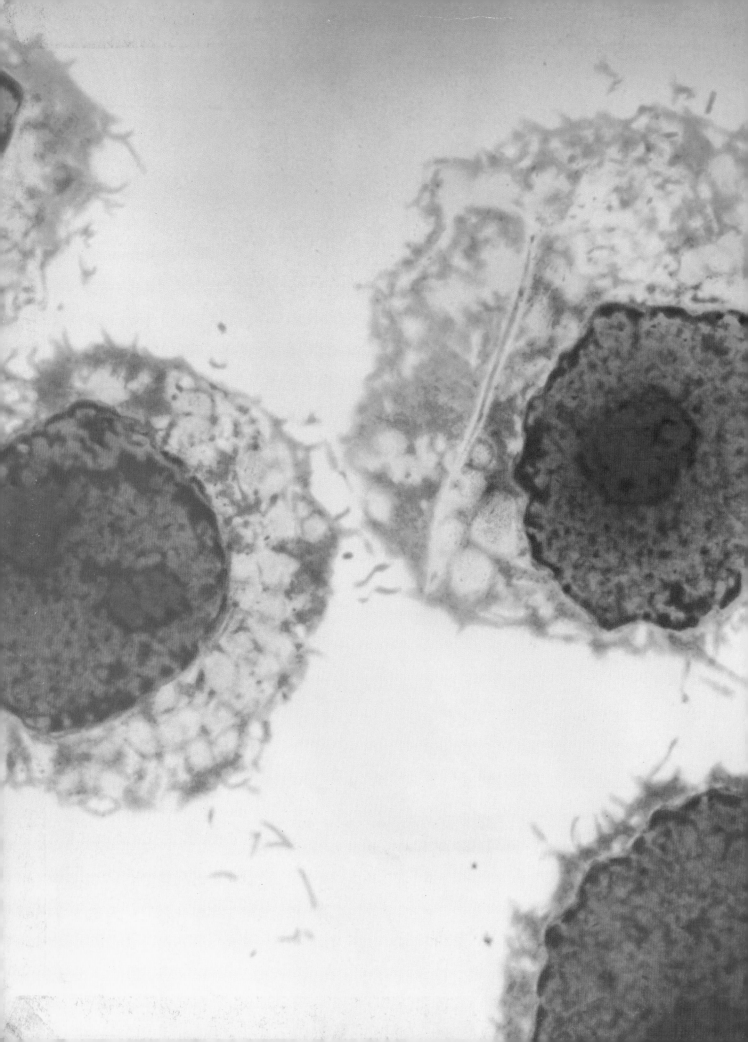